The BATTLE of WESTPORT
OCTOBER · 23 · 1864

# CIVIL WAR!

THE KANSAS CITY STAR'S CIVIL WAR 150

[ 1 ]

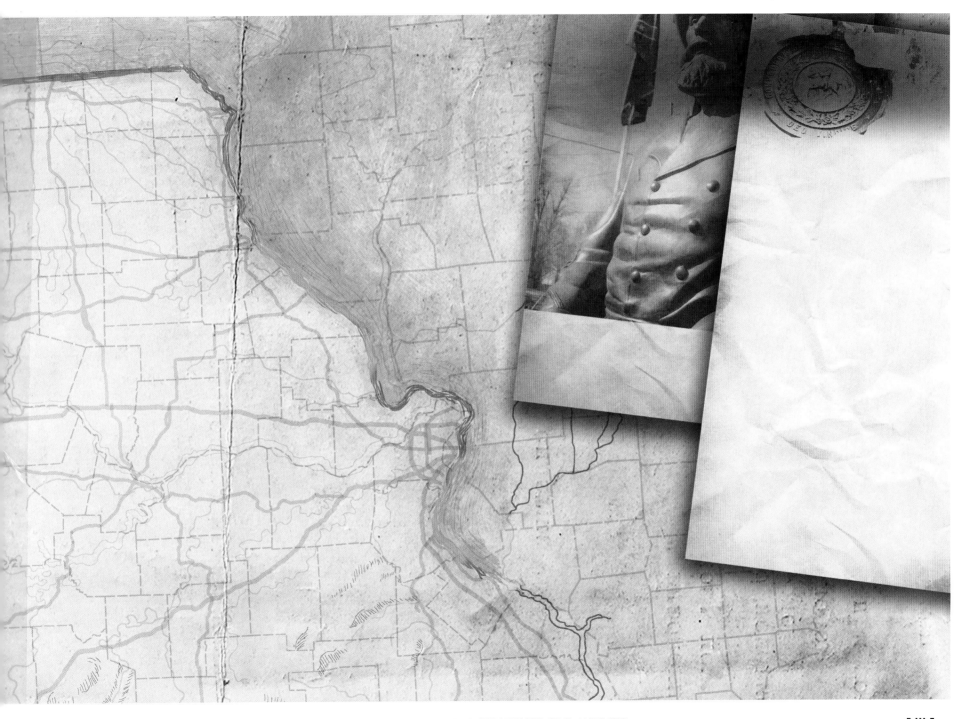

# CIVIL WAR!
## Tensions Still Divide After 150 Years

By the staff of
The Kansas City Star
Designed by Greg Branson

Published by
Kansas City Star Books
1729 Grand Blvd.
Kansas City, Missouri 64108
All rights reserved.
Copyright © 2011
by The Kansas City Star

First edition, first printing
ISBN: 978-1-61169-032-3
Library of Congress: 2011943038

Printed in the United States.

To order copies, call StarInfo at
816-234-4636 and say "operator."
www.TheKansasCityStore.com

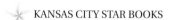

KANSAS CITY STAR BOOKS

**"Bohemian Brigade"** was the nickname Civil War correspondents gave themselves. The Star's brigade is led by national editor Darryl W. Levings (front) and staffed by (right to left) reporters Rick Montgomery, Glenn Rice, Brian Burnes and Lee Hill Kavanaugh, KansasCity.com videographers Todd Feeback and Monty Davis, reporter Mará Rose Williams and photographer Keith Myers. Missing in action are photographers Allison Long and Rich Sugg, graphic artists Dave Eames and Neil Nakahodo, and page designer Charles Gooch.

# Foreword

Delicate and full of new life, the fawn was startled from its hiding place amid the white stones studding the south St. Louis hill. The moment was enjoyed, then the search taken up again through the thousands of graves. Jefferson Barracks had been one of the Union's biggest military hospitals and, health care being what it was in those days, fed a National Cemetery of some sprawl overlooking the Mississippi.

Finally, a marker's carved words revealed the resting place of one Pvt. Orlando Levings, distant kin unknown until found on the directory of the dead. Probably brought up by steamer from Vicksburg, he died in December 1863. Taken by malaria perhaps or dysentery?

Had Orlando lived, he could have been part of Kansas City history ... of flapping regimental colors, bugle trills and the rattle of carbines. On Oct. 23, 1864, his 10th Missouri Cavalry crossed the Blue River under withering rebel fire near what is now Swope Park and crashed into Maj. Gen. Sterling Price's lines. Two days later, the 101th caught up with their old governor at Mine Creek, Kan., and helped break his army for good.

The personal discovery, made on a photo run for The Kansas City Star's Civil War coverage, balanced somewhat a family history that had leaned to the other side: Young Flavius Shortridge, who rode with guerrilla chief Col. Joe Porter until captured. Like Orlando, he died of disease, but at the Federal prison camp at Alton, just upriver.

Had it not been for The Star's commitment to the sesquicentennial of this terrible war, and my editor's role in it, I would have missed Orlando's small role but large sacrifice.

Yet, everyone at The Star who worked on our project came away with new and deeper understandings of this terrible sundering of our people. One writer was shocked to learn her ancestors had been slave holders. Another, an African American reporter, was chagrined to realize that her son, like so many others today, believed that the Civil War was tangled in states' rights, not rooted irrevocably in the old evil of slavery.

We found wonderful tales of old shames and heroics, characters and clashes of arms that needed to be reintroduced to our readers. We read their old letters, walked among their graves. And listened to Abraham Lincoln, who said, "The world will little note, nor long remember, what we say here, but it can never forget what they did here." He wasn't just talking about that Pennsylvania hillside.

He was speaking of Westport and Lexington, Wilson's Creek and Lone Jack, too. And smaller places around us, Grinter's Farm, Baxter's Springs, Glasgow and Camden Point.

Although fierce and plenty, our battles were smaller, while the massacres were good-sized and too many. Nor was it just Yankee troops versus Rebel troops here. It was neighbor against neighbor. Army regulars and enrolled militias, guerrillas and jayhawkers bled the countryside white, lit the night skies around Kansas City with torched farmsteads and towns. Hangings, firing squads and scalping became the order of the day. Hundreds of Southern women were thrown in prisons and banished from the state; thousands in four Missouri counties forced by Order No. 11 to leave nearly all behind.

So some feelings linger, our reporters found. Mostly it's pride of heritage, revived at area re-enactments, but here and there little embers of bitterness are fanned by current political winds.

For most of us, however, history has marched on. Large segments of Americans feel no — want no — connection to those old days and hard times. In some of our schools, they seem to have little more relevance than the Punic Wars. Monuments to those who stood their ground amidst the whistling minié balls are all around us, hardly considered.

This should not be. As the late Shelby Foote, writer and historian, said: "Before the war, it was said 'the United States are.' Grammatically, it was spoken that way and thought of as a collection of independent states. And after the war, it was always 'the United States is,' as we say today without being self-conscious at all. And that sums up what the war accomplished. It made us an 'is.'"

This book is dedicated to that reforging on the fires that burned around us and made us one.

— *Darryl W. Levings*

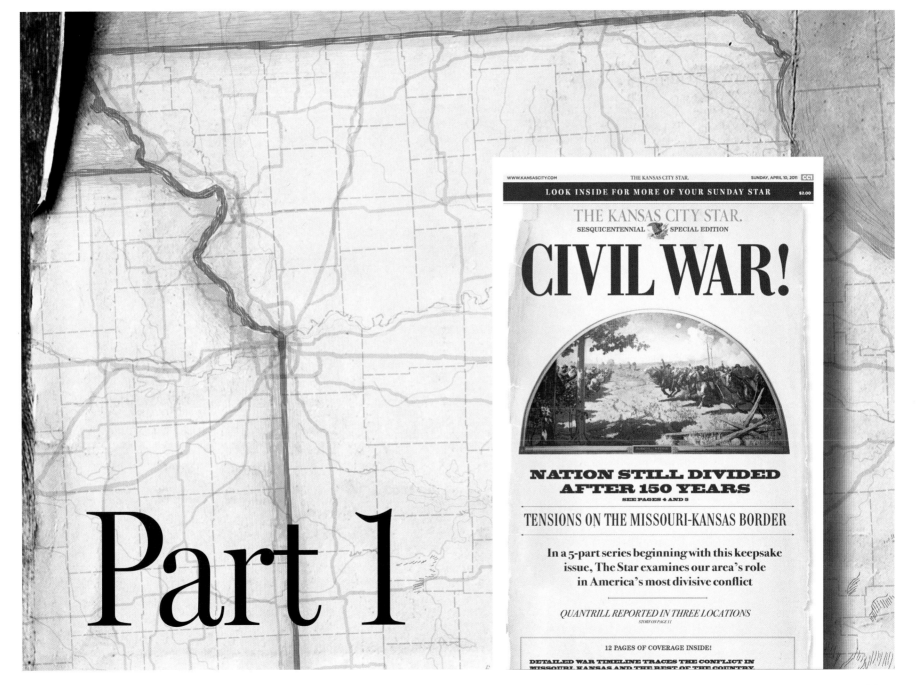

Part 1

150 years after the Civil War

# Did we really learn?

By **RICK MONTGOMERY** ★ THE KANSAS CITY STAR

At his inauguration, the eloquent but embattled president from Illinois spoke hopefully of the "mystic chords of memory" keeping Americans united.

Those chords now keep the Civil War echoing, 150 years after he, Abe Lincoln, watched it erupt.

Beginning with the April 2011 sesquicentennial of Southern cannons firing on Fort Sumter, S.C., a nation divided by some of the same arguments — about federal reach versus states' rights, about old economy versus new, about race and religion — embarked on a four-year observance of a war that rewrote most everything.

The real flashpoint predates Fort Sumter by several years, however.

**Missouri guerrillas came to Lawrence to catch Red Legs and U.S. Sen. James Lane, who slipped away. Unfortunately, between 150 and 200 other men and boys, the majority civilians, were not so fortunate in the bushwhacker killing spree.** | KANSASMEMORY.ORG, KANSAS STATE HISTORICAL SOCIETY

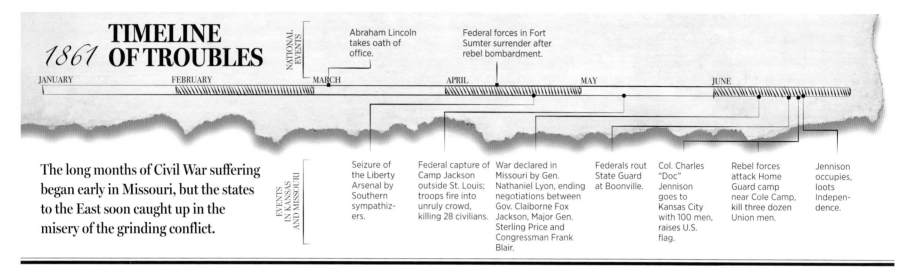

**TIMELINE**
*1861* **OF TROUBLES**

JANUARY    FEBRUARY    MARCH    APRIL    MAY    JUNE

NATIONAL EVENTS

Abraham Lincoln takes oath of office.

Federal forces in Fort Sumter surrender after rebel bombardment.

The long months of Civil War suffering began early in Missouri, but the states to the East soon caught up in the misery of the grinding conflict.

EVENTS IN KANSAS AND MISSOURI

Seizure of the Liberty Arsenal by Southern sympathizers.

Federal capture of Camp Jackson outside St. Louis; troops fire into unruly crowd, killing 28 civilians.

War declared in Missouri by Gen. Nathaniel Lyon, ending negotiations between Gov. Claiborne Fox Jackson, Major Gen. Sterling Price and Congressman Frank Blair.

Federals rout State Guard at Boonville.

Col. Charles "Doc" Jennison goes to Kansas City with 100 men, raises U.S. flag.

Rebel forces attack Home Guard camp near Cole Camp, kill three dozen Union men.

Jennison occupies, loots Independence.

And it burst in a place neither North nor South, but here — where slavery's western trajectory hit a dead end.

On the Missouri-Kansas line.

Placards hype the "Border War" that rages still, metaphorically, at sporting events between the universities of Missouri and Kansas. But history is less cute. Nowhere else were the war's hostilities more tightly coiled and personal.

"East Coast historians tell you the war started in Fort Sumter and ended at Appomattox," said Terry McConnell of Independence as a meeting of the Civil War Round Table of Western Missouri came to a close.

"Uh-uh. It started right here in 1855, and it hasn't ended."

The state line pitted neighbor against neighbor — in savage ways back then and destructive ways even now.

The bad blood only started with the question of slaveholding, which had been legal across Missouri since its statehood in 1821. Ultimately the violence would be fueled less by ideals of equality (some "free-soilers" in Kansas, in fact, argued for keeping black people out) than by vengeance and vicious one-upmanship.

Long before the U.S. wars of the 2000s, boyish-looking irregulars, bushwhackers and Red Legs — today we call them terrorists or death squads — lurked outside Kansas City.

Missourians, whether hostile or not to the Union that governed them, endured federal occupation and fiery pre-emptive strikes. At the John Brown Museum in Osawatomie, Kan., curator Grady Atwater described that landscape in the most contemporary of ways:

"This was the Iraq or Afghanistan of its day."

## LOSS OF A GENERATION

Each major anniversary of the Civil War sparks a new conversation about our direction as a nation.

Each observance forms its own narrative about memory, reconciliation and the reasons for which well more than 600,000 citizens would die. Proportional to the size of the maturing country, the body count would approach 6 million Americans today, or the entire population of modern-day Missouri.

About as many American troops would be killed in all other wars combined.

"Given the loss of a whole generation, the amazing thing is that 150 years later the country is together at all," said cultural historian Robert Thompson at Syracuse University.

"Maybe not happily, but together."

Much and little has changed. This sesquicentennial arrived with an African-American in the Oval Office. His election came earlier than anyone would have

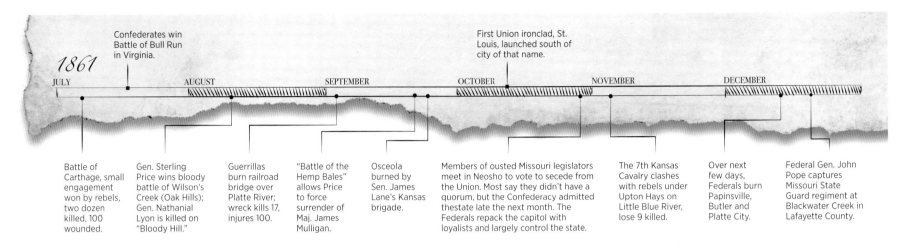

**1861**

Confederates win Battle of Bull Run in Virginia.

First Union ironclad, St. Louis, launched south of city of that name.

JULY — AUGUST — SEPTEMBER — OCTOBER — NOVEMBER — DECEMBER

Battle of Carthage, small engagement won by rebels, two dozen killed, 100 wounded.

Gen. Sterling Price wins bloody battle of Wilson's Creek (Oak Hills); Gen. Nathanial Lyon is killed on "Bloody Hill."

Guerrillas burn railroad bridge over Platte River; wreck kills 17, injures 100.

"Battle of the Hemp Bales" allows Price to force surrender of Maj. James Mulligan.

Osceola burned by Sen. James Lane's Kansas brigade.

Members of ousted Missouri legislators meet in Neosho to vote to secede from the Union. Most say they didn't have a quorum, but the Confederacy admitted the state late the next month. The Federals repack the capitol with loyalists and largely control the state.

The 7th Kansas Cavalry clashes with rebels under Upton Hays on Little Blue River, lose 9 killed.

Over next few days, Federals burn Papinsville, Butler and Platte City.

Federal Gen. John Pope captures Missouri State Guard regiment at Blackwater Creek in Lafayette County.

---

guessed during the civil-rights push of the 1960s.

In that decade, you may have observed the war's 100th anniversary. Some planning events were held at segregated hotels, making it difficult for African-Americans to attend.

Fifty years later: On issues well beyond racial equality — health care, illegal immigration, globalization, labor unions, federal spending — America sees a cleaving of opinions as deep as at any time since the 1960s.

"Those were the days when politicians from both parties supported the struggle for civil rights. Now they struggle to be civil," said activist Julian Bond, the grandson of a slave.

These days conservative commentator Mike Huckabee equates the furor over slavery to the abortion debate, both involving "the sanctity of human life" and strained constitutional interpretations.

Democrats and Republicans argue endlessly over federal income taxes — first devised by Congress to fund the Civil War.

Others bristle at globalization and unbridled change. Just as the South in the 1860s sensed an encroachment of new industries and political power from the North, many today argue that America's glory years are behind us.

Today, said University of Central Missouri historian Delia Gillis, students have heard so much about "states' rights" in their lifetimes, even the young adults of color argue the war had more to do with sovereignty than slavery.

"Narratives of what this war was about all take on a certain bias," Gillis said. "The South has been very successful having their version represented."

Especially in the South, observances of the last few months have called attention to a house yet divided:

❚ A "secession ball" in Charleston, S.C., attracted partiers in antebellum garb to celebrate the 150th an-

niversary of that state's withdrawal from the Union. Outside the dance, more than 100 protested what they interpreted as "a celebration of slavery" and a backward-looking "confederacy of the mind."

❚ A group calling itself the Texas Nationalist Movement rallied at the state Capitol to push a resolution that would allow Texans to vote this November on separating from the United States. Though Republican Gov. Rick Perry uttered the word "secession" soon after President Barack Obama's election, he said he only advocated states being allowed to break from Social Security and other federal mandates.

❚ Mississippians argued over commemorative license plates — including a design for 2014 honoring a Confederate general who later served as grand wizard of the Ku Klux Klan.

"In many ways, the Civil War still lingers," said U.S. Rep. Emanuel Cleaver, a Kansas City Democrat. "Most of the states in the Confederacy are what we call the

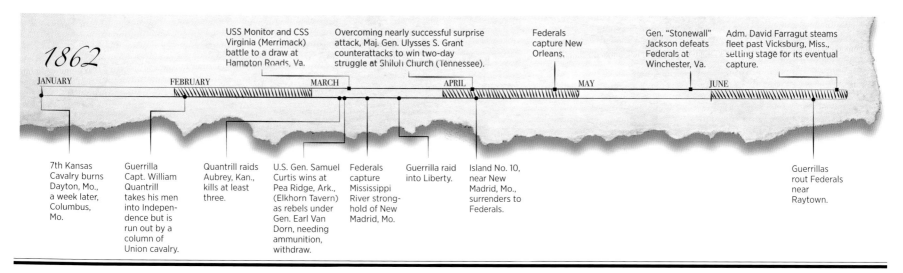

1862

JANUARY    FEBRUARY    MARCH    APRIL    MAY    JUNE

USS Monitor and CSS Virginia (Merrimack) battle to a draw at Hampton Roads, Va.

Overcoming nearly successful surprise attack, Maj. Gen. Ulysses S. Grant counterattacks to win two-day struggle at Shiloh Church (Tennessee).

Federals capture New Orleans.

Gen. "Stonewall" Jackson defeats Federals at Winchester, Va.

Adm. David Farragut steams fleet past Vicksburg, Miss., setting stage for its eventual capture.

7th Kansas Cavalry burns Dayton, Mo., a week later, Columbus, Mo.

Guerrilla Capt. William Quantrill takes his men into Independence but is run out by a column of Union cavalry.

Quantrill raids Aubrey, Kan., kills at least three.

U.S. Gen. Samuel Curtis wins at Pea Ridge, Ark., (Elkhorn Tavern) as rebels under Gen. Earl Van Dorn, needing ammunition, withdraw.

Federals capture Mississippi River stronghold of New Madrid, Mo.

Guerrilla raid into Liberty.

Island No. 10, near New Madrid, Mo., surrenders to Federals.

Guerrillas rout Federals near Raytown.

---

red states. They're the most conservative states in the Union. ...

"What was done with guns and bayonets is done today with tongues. The red-hot rhetoric in Washington, according to the old-timers here, is worse than it's ever been."

That's saying quite a bit. In maybe the most famous congressional outburst ever — ruder, even, than a representative shouting "You lie" during a presidential address — an earlier South Carolinian, Rep. Preston Brooks, used a cane to bludgeon Sen. Charles Sumner, a Massachusetts abolitionist, on the Senate floor.

That was in 1856, as emigrants from both Northern and Southern states streamed into the Kansas territory to swing its destiny.

Within five years, the Civil War was on.

## THE SLAVERY QUESTION

It got complicated, this war on the border. But a lot

boiled down to divisions we recognize today.

One side claims to be righteous, the other gets its back up. One plays dirty, the other gets dirtier.

The Missourians were here first, by 40 years. Many came from Southern states and brought their slaves along.

After Congress in 1854 allowed the slavery question in the Kansas territory to be decided by its voters, many abolitionists swooped in to claim land and impose their will on the West.

Similarly, Missourians, cast as "border ruffians" and "pukes" by the newcomers from the East, poured across the border to stuff ballot boxes with pro-slavery votes and to intimidate Kansans.

Kansas abolitionist Charles B. Stearns wrote: "When I deal with men made in God's image, I will never shoot them; but these pro-slavery Missourians are demons from the bottomless pit and may be shot with impunity."

None was more willing to do that than old John Brown — a white evangelical from New York who arrived in Kansas territory girding to die for the cause.

In May 1856, Brown and several others, including his sons, dragged five pro-slavery men — though none actually owned slaves — out of their homes near a Kansas creek called Pottawatomie. They used sabers to hack at their victims. Then the elder Brown deposited a bullet in the head of each. God's work, he believed.

Missourians along the border sent 250 men into the abolitionist stronghold of Osawatomie to burn the town down. In the fight, they killed one of Brown's sons.

So what started as an ideological split turned personal, with looting and killings back and forth.

In time the pillagers from "Bleeding Kansas" would adopt the name Jayhawkers — derived, some believe, from a fictional bird as nasty as a blue jay and hungry

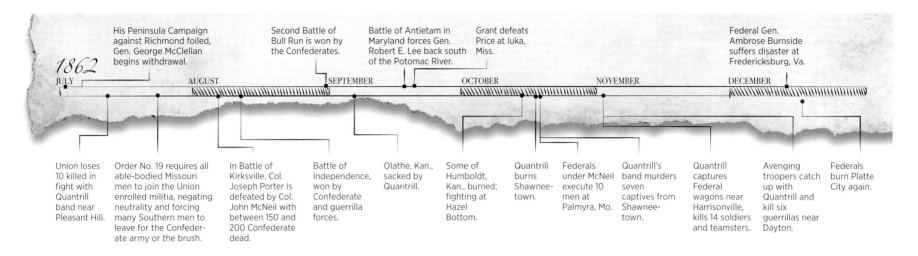

**1862**

JULY — AUGUST — SEPTEMBER — OCTOBER — NOVEMBER — DECEMBER

His Peninsula Campaign against Richmond foiled, Gen. George McClellan begins withdrawal.

Second Battle of Bull Run is won by the Confederates.

Battle of Antietam in Maryland forces Gen. Robert E. Lee back south of the Potomac River.

Grant defeats Price at Iuka, Miss.

Federal Gen. Ambrose Burnside suffers disaster at Fredericksburg, Va.

Union loses 10 killed in fight with Quantrill band near Pleasant Hill.

Order No. 19 requires all able-bodied Missouri men to join the Union enrolled militia, negating neutrality and forcing many Southern men to leave for the Confederate army or the brush.

In Battle of Kirksville, Col. Joseph Porter is defeated by Col. John McNeil with between 150 and 200 Confederate dead.

Battle of Independence, won by Confederate and guerrilla forces.

Olathe, Kan., sacked by Quantrill.

Some of Humboldt, Kan., burned; fighting at Hazel Bottom.

Quantrill burns Shawnee-town.

Federals under McNeil execute 10 men at Palmyra, Mo.

Quantrill's band murders seven captives from Shawnee-town.

Quantrill captures Federal wagons near Harrisonville, kills 14 soldiers and teamsters.

Avenging troopers catch up with Quantrill and kill six guerrillas near Dayton.

Federals burn Platte City again.

**Grady Atwater, administrator of the John Brown Museum State Historic Site in Osawatomie, Kan., showed off a cabin used by Brown as a headquarters. Of that bloody time, Atwater said: "This was the Iraq or Afghanistan of its day."**

PHOTO BY KEITH MYERS | THE KANSAS CITY STAR

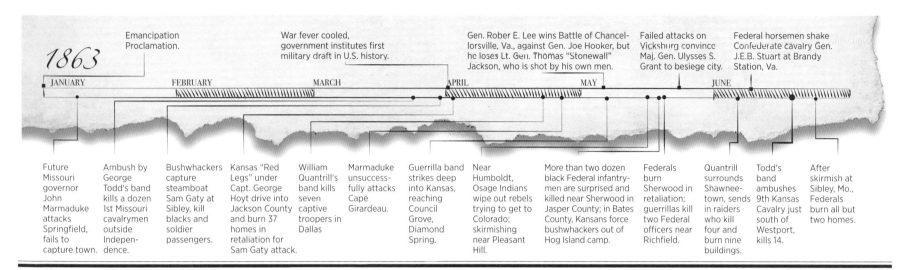

**1863**

| | | | |
|---|---|---|---|
| **JANUARY** | **FEBRUARY** | **MARCH** | **APRIL** |

Emancipation Proclamation.

War fever cooled, government institutes first military draft in U.S. history.

Gen. Rober E. Lee wins Battle of Chancellorsville, Va., against Gen. Joe Hooker, but he loses Lt. Gen. Thomas "Stonewall" Jackson, who is shot by his own men.

Failed attacks on Vicksburg convince Maj. Gen. Ulysses S. Grant to besiege city.

Federal horsemen shake Confederate cavalry Gen. J.E.B. Stuart at Brandy Station, Va.

**MAY** **JUNE**

Future Missouri governor John Marmaduke attacks Springfield, fails to capture town.

Ambush by George Todd's band kills a dozen 1st Missouri cavalrymen outside Independence.

Bushwhackers capture steamboat Sam Gaty at Sibley, kill blacks and soldier passengers.

Kansas "Red Legs" under Capt. George Hoyt drive into Jackson County and burn 37 homes in retaliation for Sam Gaty attack.

William Quantrill's band kills seven captive troopers in Dallas

Marmaduke unsuccessfully attacks Cape Girardeau.

Guerrilla band strikes deep into Kansas, reaching Council Grove, Diamond Spring.

Near Humboldt, Osage Indians wipe out rebels trying to get to Colorado; skirmishing near Pleasant Hill.

More than two dozen black Federal infantrymen are surprised and killed near Sherwood in Jasper County; in Bates County, Kansans force bushwhackers out of Hog Island camp.

Federals burn Sherwood in retaliation; guerrillas kill two Federal officers near Richfield.

Quantrill surrounds Shawneetown, sends in raiders who kill four and burn nine buildings.

Todd's band ambushes 9th Kansas Cavalry just south of Westport, kills 14.

After skirmish at Sibley, Mo., Federals burn all but two homes.

---

Civil War re-enactor and history buff Jim Beckner of Raymore, whose finished basement is filled with Civil War memorabilia, books, clothing and models, gladly studies both Union and Confederate ideologies. But others in that field of study are clearly both partisan.

PHOTO BY KEITH MYERS | THE KANSAS CITY STAR

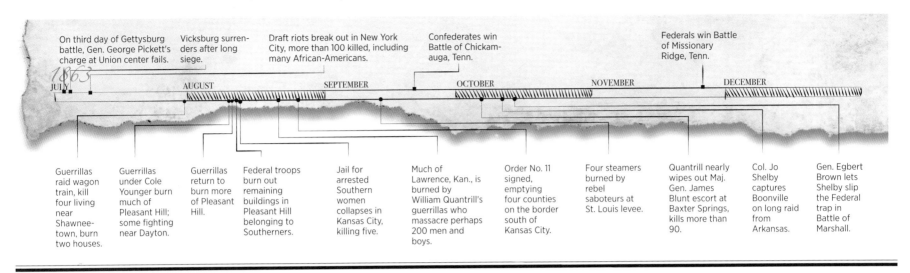

*1863*

| JULY | AUGUST | SEPTEMBER | OCTOBER | NOVEMBER | DECEMBER |

On third day of Gettysburg battle, Gen. George Pickett's charge at Union center fails.

Vicksburg surrenders after long siege.

Draft riots break out in New York City, more than 100 killed, including many African-Americans.

Confederates win Battle of Chickamauga, Tenn.

Federals win Battle of Missionary Ridge, Tenn.

Guerrillas raid wagon train, kill four living near Shawneetown, burn two houses.

Guerrillas under Cole Younger burn much of Pleasant Hill; some fighting near Dayton.

Guerrillas return to burn more of Pleasant Hill.

Federal troops burn out remaining buildings in Pleasant Hill belonging to Southerners.

Jail for arrested Southern women collapses in Kansas City, killing five.

Much of Lawrence, Kan., is burned by William Quantrill's guerrillas who massacre perhaps 200 men and boys.

Order No. 11 signed, emptying four counties on the border south of Kansas City.

Four steamers burned by rebel saboteurs at St. Louis levee.

Quantrill nearly wipes out Maj. Gen. James Blunt escort at Baxter Springs, kills more than 90.

Col. Jo Shelby captures Boonville on long raid from Arkansas.

Gen. Egbert Brown lets Shelby slip the Federal trap in Battle of Marshall.

---

as a hawk.

During the coming remembrances, local politicians had best be careful what they say.

At a performance one summer by the Kansas City Symphony in the Flint Hills, the then-governor of Kansas, Mark Parkinson, riled Missourians in the crowd with his quips about William Quantrill's 1863 sacking of Lawrence.

A letter writer to The Kansas City Star demanded an apology: "Isn't unity along our borders, today and tomorrow, what we're all striving to achieve?"

It's more of a striving never to forget, judging by attractions that dot the region.

On the Kansas side, middle-school kids in KU Jayhawk jackets sit in on lectures in Lecompton, where in 1855, pro-slavery forces penned the territory's first constitution before anti-slavery arrivals drafted their own. The historical society distributes to schools game cards to play "Bleeding Kansas Bingo," featuring images of Brown and fierce U.S. Sen. James Lane.

In Missouri, the birthplace of the bushwhacker James boys is a Kearney draw. Puppets in Independence dramatize the Border War, Harrisonville recently erected a monument to the "Burnt District," and rebel flags flap from graves in Osceola, a town wiped out by Lane and the Kansans.

"There still are people who are diehards either way," said Janet Weaver of the Gen. Sterling Price Museum in Keytesville, Mo., dedicated to the memory of the ex-governor and rebel officer who tried more than once to release the Union's tenuous grip on Missouri.

Some are offended that re-enactors in blue and gray would even wish to clash again in Missouri this year for the Battle of Lexington and the Battle of Wilson's Creek. (During that first year of the war, 40 percent of casualties nationwide and 40 percent of the battles happened in Missouri.)

But to ignore the war — "the fiery crucible," in historian William Hesseltine's words, "in which the old nation was melted down and out of which modern America was poured" — is to forget how our fiercest differences can bring our nation to annihilation's brink.

"If we haven't learned from the Civil War yet," said Terry Ramsey, curator of the popular Bushwhacker Museum in Nevada, Mo., "it's time we do."

Union Gen. John B. Sanborn recalled in 1886: "If there is anything of value to a future age to be learned ... it is that there exists in the breasts of the people of educated and Christian communities wild and ferocious passions."

He learned it serving near the Missouri-Kansas border.

"I think the bitterness on the border had to do with people not playing by rules," said Gary Nodler, an ex-legislator in southwest Missouri. "The scar tissue is deeper than what's left after a conventional war."

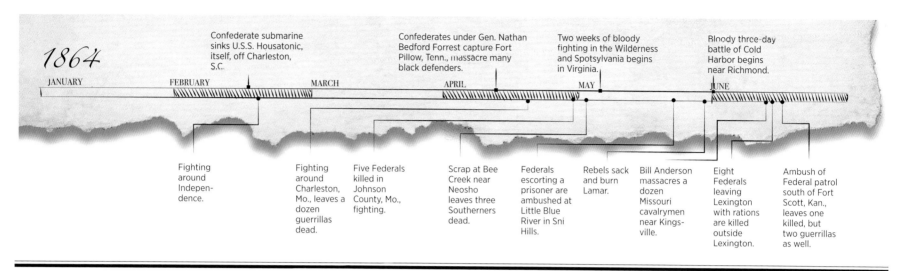

1864

JANUARY    FEBRUARY    MARCH    APRIL    MAY    JUNE

Confederate submarine sinks U.S.S. Housatonic, itself, off Charleston, S.C.

Confederates under Gen. Nathan Bedford Forrest capture Fort Pillow, Tenn., massacre many black defenders.

Two weeks of bloody fighting in the Wilderness and Spotsylvania begins in Virginia.

Bloody three-day battle of Cold Harbor begins near Richmond.

Fighting around Independence.

Fighting around Charleston, Mo., leaves a dozen guerrillas dead.

Five Federals killed in Johnson County, Mo., fighting.

Scrap at Bee Creek near Neosho leaves three Southerners dead.

Federals escorting a prisoner are ambushed at Little Blue River in Sni Hills.

Rebels sack and burn Lamar.

Bill Anderson massacres a dozen Missouri cavalrymen near Kingsville.

Eight Federals leaving Lexington with rations are killed outside Lexington.

Ambush of Federal patrol south of Fort Scott, Kan., leaves one killed, but two guerrillas as well.

## GENERAL ORDER NO. 11

Tom Rafiner's obsession is typical.

Retired from the insurance line, Rafiner, of Parkville, wanted to devote some time to genealogy. He learned that a couple of ancestors lived in Cass County when the war began, but the records seemed to have vanished, 1,700 households erased from memory.

So began Rafiner's six-year fixation on an episode he never learned in history class: General Order No. 11, issued in 1863 by Union Gen. Thomas Ewing in Kansas City, reduced to ash the homes and livelihoods of thousands of residents of Cass and three other counties on Missouri's western edge.

The eradication happened in response to Quantrill's raid, in which perhaps 200 Lawrence men and boys were slaughtered — by far the bloodiest act of domestic terrorism until Timothy McVeigh bombed an Oklahoma City federal building in 1995.

Rural Missourians along the western border, suspected of feeding and sheltering the guerrillas, were given 15 days to gather up belongings and scram. Much of their livestock was stolen and several of their towns were torched by Kansas marauders. Order No. 11 just finished off what was left.

The devastation was immortalized in a painting by Missouri artist George Caleb Bing-ham, whose hatred of Ewing was intense.

The hostility lingers for many longtime families of Cass, rural Jackson, Bates and part of Vernon counties.

"I spoke with a man in Lone Jack who said he knew which family assassinated his great-grandfather," said Rafiner, whose research led to a book about Cass County's loss, "Caught Between Three Fires."

"He tells me, 'And I know where they live.' Not lived, but where they still live. ...

"I heard another man say he doesn't even drive into Kansas," Rafiner said. "Jeesh, it's been 150 years!"

Writers and homegrown historians sense a different vibe when giving Civil War lectures in the Sunflower State.

"In Lawrence, they know all about Quantrill, but they really don't know about Order 11," said Judy Billings of the city's tourism bureau. "Yes, Kansans bled. But so did Missourians."

In Jackson County, Union troops pillaged the home of Solomon and Harriet Louisa Young, grandparents to Harry Truman. In 1906, his grandmother won a $3,800 settlement from the U.S. government to cover property looted or destroyed.

She never forgot. Recalling how he proudly wore his new Missouri National Guard uniform into her home, Truman later wrote: "She said, 'Harry, this is the first time since 1863 that a blue uniform has been in this house. Don't bring it here again.'

"I didn't."

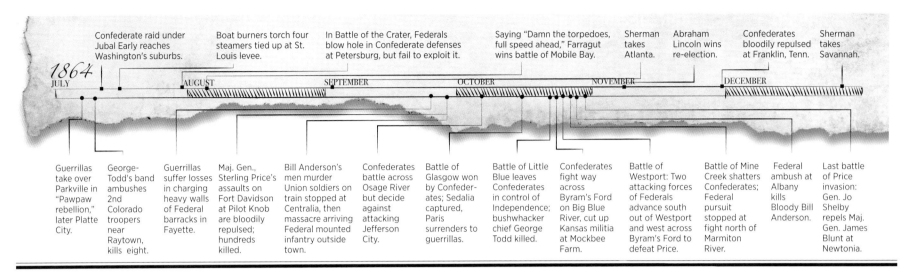

*1864*

JULY — AUGUST — SEPTEMBER — OCTOBER — NOVEMBER — DECEMBER

Confederate raid under Jubal Early reaches Washington's suburbs.

Boat burners torch four steamers tied up at St. Louis levee.

In Battle of the Crater, Federals blow hole in Confederate defenses at Petersburg, but fail to exploit it.

Saying "Damn the torpedoes, full speed ahead," Farragut wins battle of Mobile Bay.

Sherman takes Atlanta.

Abraham Lincoln wins re-election.

Confederates bloodily repulsed at Franklin, Tenn.

Sherman takes Savannah.

Guerrillas take over Parkville in "Pawpaw rebellion," later Platte City.

George-Todd's band ambushes 2nd Colorado troopers near Raytown, kills eight.

Guerrillas suffer losses in charging heavy walls of Federal barracks in Fayette.

Maj. Gen., Sterling Price's assaults on Fort Davidson at Pilot Knob are bloodily repulsed; hundreds killed.

Bill Anderson's men murder Union soldiers on train stopped at Centralia, then massacre arriving Federal mounted infantry outside town.

Confederates battle across Osage River but decide against attacking Jefferson City.

Battle of Glasgow won by Confederates; Sedalia captured, Paris surrenders to guerrillas.

Battle of Little Blue leaves Confederates in control of Independence; bushwhacker chief George Todd killed.

Confederates fight way across Byram's Ford on Big Blue River, cut up Kansas militia at Mockbee Farm.

Battle of Westport: Two attacking forces of Federals advance south out of Westport and west across Byram's Ford to defeat Price.

Battle of Mine Creek shatters Confederates; Federal pursuit stopped at fight north of Marmiton River.

Federal ambush at Albany kills Bloody Bill Anderson.

Last battle of Price invasion: Gen. Jo Shelby repels Maj. Gen. James Blunt at Newtonia.

## A NATIONAL HERITAGE AREA

Twelve years ago, Billings, of Lawrence, and about a dozen other Kansans — plus a lone Missourian from the Bushwhacker Museum — gathered to brainstorm ways to promote the 150th anniversary of the 1854 establishment of the Kansas territory.

Their focus was Bleeding Kansas — the name they'd propose to Congress in seeking a special designation as a national heritage area.

Then-congressman Jim Talent wanted 12 Missouri counties thrown into the heritage area. Ike Skelton, the former congressman to the state's 4th District, would approve the measure only if the name "Bleeding Kansas" was dropped.

Back in Lawrence, heated meetings drove some Kansans off the planning committee.

Finally, organizers agreed on the boundaries and mission of "Freedom's Frontier."

The heritage area encompasses 41 counties. Its management plan is to establish the region as "a testing ground for debates concerning rights, freedom and their meaning in the American democracy."

Billings: "Interconnectedness is definitely our goal."

As Civil War observances roll out, the question remains whether visitors care much about "interconnectedness." Many would rather stick to their own points of view about who, in all the bloodletting, was good and who was bad, said Atwater at the John Brown Museum.

"People from Europe who visit us pretty much consider Brown a hero," Atwater said.

Americans, he said, tend to have their minds set when they walk in the door, and many will argue that Brown was an 1850s version of Osama bin Laden, a bloodthirsty villain driven by religious extremism.

"Both sides," the curator said, "were equally monstrous."

## ROUND TABLE-GO-ROUND

Any year, sesquicentennial or otherwise, dozens of shows and discussions are open to Civil War buffs on either side of the border.

"I will not stand for this nation to be torn asunder!" cried a Johnson County, Mo., computer programmer-turned-actor before crumpling from gunshot wounds beneath the wooden chandeliers of the old courthouse in Warrensburg.

There, a cast of about 20 performed "Murder in the Courthouse" on the anniversary of a politically charged killing during a February 1861 election.

In the audience sat Jim Beckner of Raymore.

A longtime buff with a white beard and gentle manner, Beckner will attest to being "very unusual" in that he happily crisscrosses the state line to absorb varying ideologies.

Three nights after watching the play in central Missouri — where a secessionist on stage declared, "Every

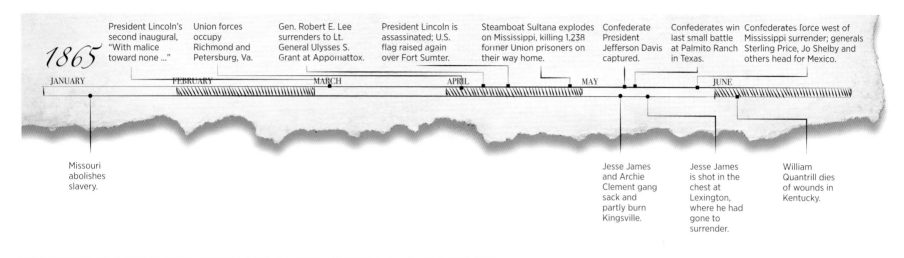

1865

| JANUARY | FEBRUARY | MARCH | APRIL | MAY | JUNE |

**President Lincoln's second inaugural,** "With malice toward none ..."

**Union forces occupy Richmond and Petersburg, Va.**

**Gen. Robert E. Lee surrenders to Lt. General Ulysses S. Grant at Appomattox.**

**President Lincoln is assassinated; U.S. flag raised again over Fort Sumter.**

**Steamboat Sultana explodes on Mississippi, killing 1,238 former Union prisoners on their way home.**

**Confederate President Jefferson Davis captured.**

**Confederates win last small battle at Palmito Ranch in Texas.**

**Confederates force west of Mississippi surrender; generals Sterling Price, Jo Shelby and others head for Mexico.**

**Missouri abolishes slavery.**

**Jesse James and Archie Clement gang sack and partly burn Kingsville.**

**Jesse James is shot in the chest at Lexington, where he had gone to surrender.**

**William Quantrill dies of wounds in Kentucky.**

Kansan that walks on two legs can go to the devil" — Beckner was dining with the enemy, mostly Kansans in Prairie Village, for a meeting of the Civil War Round Table of Kansas City.

Founded in 1958, it was the area's premier round table before some members seceded a generation ago to form a Missouri-based group.

The breakaway Round Table of Western Missouri now meets in eastern Independence. President Mike Calvert said he was inclined to "side more with the Confederate story," at least as it treats the border war.

Social considerations, too, factored into the split. Missourians grew weary of the trip to a Kansas suburb to spend $25 for a country-club meal.

By contrast, a recent meeting of Calvert's group had members tossing their coats on a billiards table and munching on home-baked brownies for an episode of Ken Burns' PBS series of the Civil War.

Yet another splinter group convenes monthly on In-dependence Square. And 20 miles due south, the Cass County Civil War Round Table has been meeting for about a decade.

Beckner involves himself in all. For more than 30 years he also has been a re-enactor at mock battles.

"We've always had trouble in Missouri getting people to wear the blue. They're all rebel-minded," he said. "We'd have 40 to 45 Confederate cavalry men versus 10 or 12 on the Union side. It was ridiculous."

For his part, Beckner has a closet stuffed with uniforms both gray and blue. The Missouri Humanities Council, which last year honored him for community achievement, called Beckner "the go-to guy for all things Civil War."

Acknowledging that the Mo-Kan divide still exists, Billings of Freedom's Frontier said: "We shouldn't be talking just two perspectives, but every perspective you can think of."

African-American, Native American, rural and urban,

all of the family histories, "basically, the development of a nation," she said. "It's about respecting them all."

Toward that aim, give credit to Bates County, Mo. A few years ago its citizens — 97 percent white, a third older than 50 — unveiled a memorial outside the county courthouse in Butler, once burned by the Yankees.

Look at the uniform — it's of an unidentified Union soldier, from Kansas.

Look closer. He's black.

The statue recognizes a little-known watershed of our nation's history. Outside of town at a place known as Island Mound, America's first black uniformed infantry-men fought for their country. And won.

## MODERN-DAY BORDER WAR

When the nation observed the 50th anniversary of the Battle of Gettysburg in 1913, Confederate and Union veterans shook hands on hallowed ground.

Similar gestures of reconciliation took place here.

Missouri Tigers free-throw shooters not only had a rowdy KU student section to deal with in a 2009 game, but John Brown as well. A sign depicted him with an NCAA trophy in his left hand. | RICH SUGG, THE KANSAS CITY STAR

"I'm proud to say that now my warmest friends are those who wore the blue, some of whom I met on the battlefield," wrote Columbus C. Blankenbecker, who fought with Price at Wilson's Creek.

The two states did not waste time finding something on which to agree: Making money beat fighting.

In Kansas City, business and political leaders of Southern and Northern persuasion buried their differences to court railroad interests. The city rebounded mightily after the Hannibal Bridge became the first permanent span of the Missouri River.

Southern folk, however, gravitated to neighborhoods east of Main, on streets named for trees. Northerners preferred Quality Hill.

A Protestant populism bonded rural reaches straddling the border, and Carrie Nation — reared in a slaveholding family in Belton — teamed with Kansas women to smash saloons.

Kansas, for decades, would be a dry state. But Missouri would be wet.

Kansas would be Republican. Missouri, for decades, would be Democrat.

Kansas regarded itself a land of freedom, as thousands of black "Exodusters" answered the call of "Ho for Kansas!" The state's high schools and public universities — unlike Missouri's — were racially integrated, allowing the aspiring botanist George Washington Carver, born to slavery in Missouri, to earn a diploma in Minneapolis, Kan.

Though blacks never exceeded 8 percent of the Kansas population, the state wielded a "symbolic power" well into the 20th century as a "testing ground" for equal rights, wrote University of Kansas historian Kim Warren in her 2010 book, "Quest for Citizenship: African and Native American Education in Kansas."

Before that testing ground would extend to fights over abortion and evolution, Kansas would be ground zero in the schooling of black children.

The U.S. Supreme Court's 1954 ruling in Brown v. Topeka Board of Education found that separation itself violated the rights of minority children.

What followed? In Kansas City, the Missouri-Kansas border erupted again. White families east of it crossed over in droves to attend white schools. And deeds in many of the new Kansas subdivisions for years kept people of color out.

You know the rest. The once-rural outback of Johnson County, Kan. — largely developed by J.C. Nichols, an Olathe native and University of Kansas graduate — bleeds the Missouri side of families, business and tax dollars to this day.

In March 2011, Missourians and Kansans converged where a Union jail collapsed in 1863, killing five Missouri women of bushwhacker families.

Now the place is the Sprint Center; the occasion the Big 12 basketball tourney. Black-clad Mizzou fans swarming a restaurant knew the talking points in their rivalry with the Jay-hawks.

"They seem to think they're superior," said Justin Scheidt of Lee's Summit.

Where Kansas fans gathered to the north, a financial planner scoffed: "In basketball, we've got a pretty good history, don't we?"

Civil enough. But also a bit spooky, since his name was John Brown.

# UNDER RIVALRY LIES COMMON GROUND

**The teams from Mizzou and KU have mascots with a heritage dating to the Civil War. But the Tigers' tale has a surprising twist.**

By RICK MONTGOMERY
The Kansas City Star

Bizarre as the bird looks, the origins of the University of Kansas mascot are pretty clear.

"Jayhawkers" were bands of free-state Kansans who looted their neighbors, like hawks stealing from a nest, in the run-up to the Civil War. Once the Union started recruiting, a Kansas regiment led by Charles Jennison adopted the nickname Jennison's Jayhawkers.

The story of the Missouri Tigers, however, is murkier, its links to the war less renowned.

Confederate troops under Gen. Sterling Price? Yankees who occupied the Columbia campus? Any and all enemies of Jay-hawks?

No, no and no.

A history teacher for Columbia Public Schools, Tom Prater, has traced the Missouri mascot to a war-era "home guard" called the Columbia Tiger Co. Some 90 men assembled to protect the township — not from jayhawkers, but from fellow Missourians determined to win one for the Confederacy.

The Columbia Tigers were local residents and businesspeople just trying to hang on to their livelihoods, Prater said.

In the fall of 1864, rumors were wild that Confederate Gen. Sterling Price's invasion army would strike at Columbia, where the lone building representing the college, Academic Hall, was held by Union forces and served as a prison for Southern sympathizers.

Anti-Union guerrillas led by William "Bloody Bill" Anderson were on a tear on the north side of the river.

So the Columbia Tigers organized, built a log bunkhouse and erected a big bell to warn the

citizenry.

"They dug a moat around the county courthouse," said Prater. "Apparently the Tigers succeeded because the guerrillas never showed up."

If their legacy lacks battlefield drama, the Tigers were proud enough to be written up in the 1882 book "History of Boone County, Missouri." In the following decade, newspapers chronicled their lobbying of the University of Missouri to be the namesake of its new football team.

Prater wanted Columbia to erect a marker at Eighth Street and Broadway, where the group's protective "Tigers' Den" bunkhouse stood back then.

Of course, history's irony — more than a century into this "Border War" hype between Missouri and Kansas sports teams — is that these Yankee Tigers never met the Yankee Jayhawks.

# Proud defiance tests the limits of reconciliation

People of the Kansas City area can be forgiven for wondering whether the Civil War actually ever ended.

To be sure, the decade-long conflict near the Missouri-Kansas border did finally burn itself out in 1865. Yet unlike other parts of America, where the war ended and soldiers marched back to homes hundreds of miles away, the combatants here largely stayed put, neighbors bound by a bloody history that shadowed them the rest of their days.

The hard feelings between modern-day partisans, however real or contrived, beg the question: Are Missourians and Kansans doomed by history to remain forever at odds?

## AUTHOR'S ESSAY

Jeremy Neely wrote "The Border Between Them: Violence and Reconciliation on the Kansas-Missouri Line." The Missouri native, who holds a doctorate in history from the University of Missouri, lives in rural Dade County, 30 miles from the state line.

The post-Civil War history of this area suggests not. A great many border war survivors reached the twilight of their lives eager to reconcile with wartime foes and leave old antagonisms buried in the past.

One reason: Business and civic leaders saw that reconciliation made good business sense. They feared that the area's reputation for violence would scare away potential immigrants and investors. Convinced that there was nothing to be gained by dwelling upon the border's dark past, boosters shifted public attention toward the area's bright prospects.

"When I laid down my musket, I considered the war at an end," said one former Confederate. "The past is behind us, our duty is to the future and as patriotic Americans we should turn our eyes in that direction."

Passage of time helped. Wartime passions and grievances were often too raw in the decade after the war, but by the 1880s a spirit of grace drew together a growing number of Civil War veterans.

Touched by what Abraham Lincoln had once called the "better angels of our nature," former combatants became central figures in the drama of postwar reconciliation.

Decoration Day, the observance we now call Memorial Day, provided the public stage for this poignant spectacle.

"The sight of Federal soldiers decorating with flowers the

graves of Confederate dead, and vice versa, against whom they had fought so hard, was often witnessed," reported one Harrisonville editor in 1889. "So great and sublime a thought was such forgiveness that it made our own petty trials sink into insignificance by comparison."

This swelling chorus of reconciliation led to careful recall of history by local boosters. Wartime hardships and the difficult questions of slavery and secession often became taboo subjects, sure to offend partisans on either side.

To render a history that was accessible to Unionists and Confederates alike, proponents of reunion stripped the war of moral judgments. Neither North nor the South had been wrong, as it went, but both had proudly reunited under one flag, redeemed by the valor and sacrifice of honored veterans.

White citizens gladly celebrated the preservation of the Union but were largely silent about the war's other central legacy, the emancipation of millions of African-American slaves. Black veterans in Kansas and Missouri typically were not invited to participate in Decoration Day programs.

Such oversights and exclusions bespoke the tragic failures of Reconstruction and the Jim Crow era that followed.

The proud defiance of some likewise tested the limits of reconciliation. The United Daughters of the Confederacy challenged the boosters' retelling of the border war by publishing unvarnished accounts of wartime misery and jayhawker depredations.

"Isn't this a part of the history of the Civil war?" asked Mrs. N.M. Harris. "Does any historian spare Quantrill?"

Guerrilla leader William Quantrill remained the border war's most polarizing figure long past his 1865 death. Beginning in 1898, many of the men who rode with Quant-

FROM "THE SOLDIER IN OUR CIVIL WAR," COURTESY OF THE KANSAS CITY LIBRARY

**Not yet part of the Confederate army, the Missouri State Guard besieged Union forces just northeast of Lexington in September 1861. When the rebels decided to create a moving breastwork of hemp bales, the battle quickly came to a close.**

rill, including Frank James and Cole Younger, gathered at Jackson County homesteads for a series of yearly reunions that laid bare some fierce differences.

Many Missourians rallied behind the Quantrill men, heralding their past efforts as protectors against hostile Kansans and federal occupiers.

The Kansas City World noted that the retired guerrillas

had settled into lives of quiet respectability, becoming "as patriotic, home-loving and peaceable a set of men as could be found anywhere."

The Quantrill men even invited Union veterans to participate in their late-summer picnics. No evidence suggests that the offer was ever accepted.

It was no coincidence that several reunions were scheduled on or near Aug. 21 — the anniversary of the Lawrence raid. News of these gatherings outraged Kansans, especially survivors of the 1863 slaughter.

Concluded George Martin: "The Quantrill reunions are the last wrigglings of the dying snake's tail."

Former guerrillas, however, were unrepentant for their part in the border war. Kit Dalton described the Lawrence massacre was "butchery of the bloodiest sort" but defended it as a "just punishment" for jayhawker provocations.

Later generations faced a choice between two broad memories of the border struggle.

The first, of the tenuous peace between the two states, can be easily lost amid the hysteria of the modern "Border War" sports rivalry.

The other, of stubborn divisions undiminished by time, comes to mind more easily.

Embers of hostility still smolder, fueling a Civil War that continues in memory if not in fact — often yielding more heat than light.

## LETTER TO A SISTER:
# 'IF I COULD ONLY BE WITH YOU A FEW DAYS'

*In early 1864, Susan Staples, an Independence widow, wrote to her sister about her troubles, from sickness in the family to ill treatment by the Federal military in the area. She particularly notes the brutal actions of 5th Missouri State Militia Col. William Penick, a former St. Joseph druggist and radical Union man who liked to say Jackson County could be tamed "if hemp, fire and gunpowder were freely used." The murdered Dr. Lee, actually Pleasant Lea, was whom Lee's Summit may be named for.*

*Here she writes her sister Mary from Independence.*

Mo Feb 1

My Dear Sister,

With a heavy, heavy, heaviest and broken spirit I attempt to write you a brief letter. You should not think hard of me for not writing to you oftener for if you knew the trials under which we labor you would not expect me to write. This leaves my family well with the exception of colds. Mother's health is not very good. She is fleshier than common but complains a good deal. She has quite a hard time as her servants are all in Coopper (Cooper County?). Felix's health is better than it has been. The Doctors say his lungs are ceriously effected. He is using Cod Liver Oil and has been since last fall. ...

Mary, I suppose that you have herd of Mr. Field's death. He died on the 17 of Oct. His death was of a very distressin nature. That awful Cancer killed him. It eat his face from his cheek bones clear down to his breast bone entirely up. It destroyed his upper and lower jawbone entirely. It also destroyed his swallow. He did not swallow one bite nor speak a word for nine days and nights. He was buried in Independence. ...

Col. Pennic's Command is stationed at Independence. He deals very strict with southerners. He has a great many female prisoners and says that he is going to bannish every lady that has husbands in the Southern Army or with the bushwhackers. He has already bannished sevral. I will tell of one or more Mrs. Tal Parrish, Mrs. Cox, the widow Haller, the widow Bagby, and a great many more. He hung a southern man the other day in old Billy Liggitt's Barn. He has hung Sam Wear and several others. He has made every Lady that has been in town for the last three months take the Oath of Allegiance. His men burned 15 houses last Friday and says he intends to burn every house that a bushwhacker has ever been in. These houses were in Dr. Lee's neighbourhood. The Federals killed Dr. Lee.

Oh Mary it is useless for me to try to tell you what Jackson County has to endure on paper but if I could only be with you a few days I could tell you something. The negroes have all left in a great measure and those that has not is so impudent that there is no living with them. Good of every kind are extremely high. Tom and I went to Kansas Citty last week. We found goods equally as high there as here but a better assortment. We have all been so dreadfully Jayhawked that I cannot tell what is to become of my children but as God has prommised to feed the young ravens who cry to him for help I hope he will in mercy remember my poor Fatherless Children....

My love to Mrs. Robbert Mason and receive a double portion for yourself. You must try and come down this spring. Write to me and believe ever to be your devoted Sister untill death.

Susan A. Staples

**Courtesy of the State Historical Society of Missouri Research Center-Kansas City**

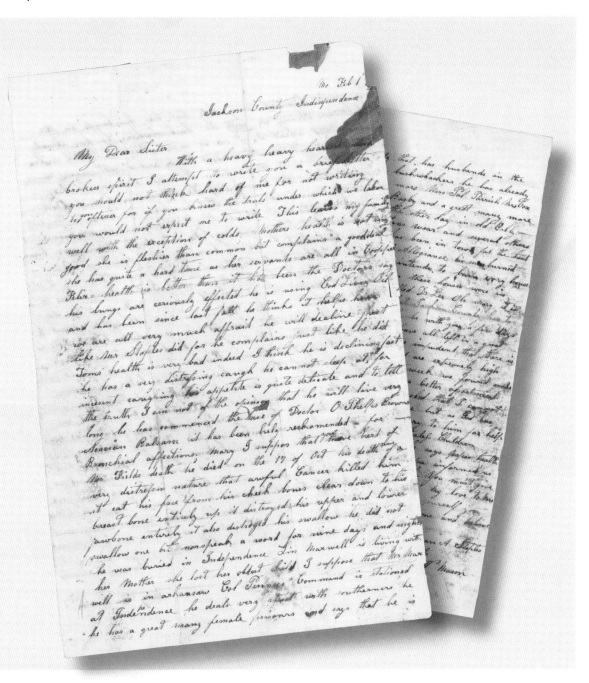

## LETTER TO A WIFE:

# 'YOU SEE HOW EVERYTHING IS MIXED UP'

*John Brown Jr. served as a Union captain of Company K, in what was originally the First Kansas Cavalry but was redesignated the Seventh, under Col. Charles "Doc" Jennison. Though a son of the martyred abolitionist who swept through Kansas before the Civil War, the younger Brown recoiled at some of his father's methods. Brown's regiment spent months in Missouri, where its actions — jayhawking, burning and killing — left deep bitterness. After less than a year, he resigned his commission and returned to Ohio, where he died in 1895.*

*Here, he writes in early 1862 to his wife, Wealthy, from Camp Johnson near Morristown, Mo.*

Wednesday evening, Jan 22

My Own Precious Wife,

It is now nearly dark — weather still mild and O how muddy.

Everywhere about camp you step in — and unless corn husks or some old hay can be got, the horses are obliged to live in the mud. Major (a horse) during the fore part of the winter had the distemper and got very poor, but is now in good condition. I think he knew me (upon Brown's return to the camp).

Tiger the dog did not at first know me, but next day he came to me with all his accustomed zeal. He is a most excellent watchdog. The Company think they couldn't get along without him.

Nothing new today but the news that a good Union man living a few miles from here had his house surrounded by a gang of rebels and he was shot. He was an old man.

Small bands or rebels are still hanging around. They get together and do up their infernal work and then go home, where if found are good Union Men. It is hard to get the kind of evidence necessary to make a clear case.

If some of those should get killed who are least deserving it would be no wonder. You see how everything is mixed up here.

I don't yet know how soon we shall go South. We are in hopes of getting Sharps Rifles for each of the Company before we leave. But all these things are matters of uncertainty.

A camp of soldiers remote from any reliable sources of news is a place where all manner of rumors are afloat. I have not seen a paper for many days and that was ten days old. We don't know what has occurred during the past two weeks in the world outside Camp Johnson.

You might like to know how it looks in my tent just now. I am writing with my writing case on my lap. Mr. Knowlton is holding the candle — next to him sits Sgt. Peck and next to him Merrick Pulsipher with the same honest good-natured face — has a feather in the left side of his cap. His beard has grown finely and his face is fairly round.

Orderly Cotton come next, he sits close by the door telling stories. Lieut. Bostwick is lying on my trunk talking. Truman Creesey has just come in with some parched corn in his hand. He sits down in the door saying, "Well, I believe I guess I'll be door keeper in the house of the Lord." ...

(Son) Johnny, I have thought of you a great many times today. Don't forget me my dear boy. ...

I want to say to Mr. Pulsipher's folks that I am fully convinced that Merrick maintains his integrity in spite of all the unfavorable circumstances with which he is surrounded. He is strict in doing all his duty and neither drinks, smokes or swears. But in all respects conducts himself like a man.

Well, once more I must say good bye. My own precious wife, my Johnny and all. Good bye. Yours always John.

**Courtesy of KansasMemory.org, Kansas State Historical Society**

# Lawrence Raid still fresh in family memory

By **RICK MONTGOMERY** ★ THE KANSAS CITY STAR

GENERATIONS
A series of family memories about local ancestors in the Civil War.

LAWRENCE | Pat Kehde works in a bookstore just two blocks from the spot. The horror that visited Seventh and Vermont streets, where her great-grandparents once lived, is nowhere evident today. The public library stands there, full of novels that strive for the kind of drama all too real for Kehde's ancestors, the Dixes:

*Rousted at dawn from the house, Jetta Dix grabs her husband's arm as marauders on horseback threaten to shoot him.*

*The wife won't let go. She begs: "Oh my God, Ralph, have you given yourself up as a prisoner? Why did you do it? I know they will kill you."*

*These terrorists will not kill women. But men are dying all around.*

*So Jetta, walking sideways, clings to Ralph as he is ordered to cross the street. She slaps at a tormentor's horse that tries to nudge her aside.*

*Then she trips on a pile of rocks. She lets go. Bang! Ralph Dix gets it in the back.*

Accounts of the carriage maker's death in the 1863 sacking of Lawrence traveled down the bloodline

Pat Kehde marvels at the resilience of her great-grandmother Jetta Dix (seen in photo), widowed during Quantrill's Raid on Lawrence in 1863. Dix and her three children were left to rebuild among the ashes. | TODD FEEBACK, THE KANSAS CITY STAR

of the widow Dix. For Kehde, Missouri guerrilla William Clarke Quantrill's August raid on the town, an abolitionist stronghold, is more than a violent chapter in history. She tries to imagine the victims up close — because they're family and friends of family — and she ascribes to them the fears, flaws and struggles of regular people.

"I think Ralph just came out here to pursue a business — a thriving business of 22 employees," Kehde said of the carriage and wagon operations on the ground floor of the three-story Dix home. "Because now we focus on the politics of the time ... we tend to think of the players as either fire-breathing abolitionists or fire-breathing slaveholders. We don't think of all these regular people caught in the crossfire."

Ralph Dix was 24 when he traveled from Connecticut to the new Kansas territory, 29 when he married Jetta, 32 when he was murdered.

An 1855 letter he wrote after coming to Lawrence made only a passing reference to the explosive politics.

"I suppose you have heard what a Time we had in the Election," Dix told his cousin.

But he withheld judgment on the activities of thousands of Missourians who staked claims in Kansas just to vote. They initially succeeded in electing a pro-slavery slate of leaders who, Dix wrote, "expect to do as they choos (sic). I don't know but they may — that remains to be seen."

Katie Armitage, author of a book on the Civil War raid — which left Lawrence incinerated and at least 150 men and teenage boys dead — said most of the victims were just folks, not fighters: "They were not expecting to be in a massacre."

Thomas Goodrich's book "Bloody Dawn" recounted Jetta Dix's frantic efforts, as Quantrill's Raiders galloped into town, to persuade her husband, his brother Steve and several employees to take cover.

She hid her three young children in a coal shed and

---

*"Can you imagine? Here was Jetta — widowed in her 20s, house destroyed, with a 3-year-old son and twin girls 20 months old. She had nobody to fall back on. I think she just said, 'I've nowhere to go, so I'm going to stay here.' What else you going to do?"*

---

discovered their nurse had locked herself in a closet.

The terrified nurse refused Jetta's pleas to come out and to mind the children. So Jetta grabbed a cleaver and hacked open the door.

As the shooting spread, Jetta saw Steve Dix tumble with a fatal gunshot wound.

And then Ralph, on his own, chose to surrender.

By the account of resident H.M. Simpson, in a letter to a friend several days after the massacre, "Mr. Dix purchased his life by paying $1,000. As soon as the money was handed over he was killed."

Many other details were provided 50 years later by Jetta, in a first-person account published in a magazine for the silver anniversary.

She had her home rebuilt, and it stood for a century. She remarried, left him for cruelty and married again, residing in Lawrence all the while.

"She'd have no grass growing under her feet — no way," Kehde said, admiring a portrait of her great-grandma grinning.

"Can you imagine? Here was Jetta — widowed in her 20s, house destroyed, with a 3-yearold son and twin girls 20 months old," Kehde said. "She had nobody to fall back on. I think she just said, 'I've nowhere to go, so I'm going to stay here.' What else you going to do? There's no paved highway heading out of town."

One of Jetta's twin daughters, Isabella, married George Edwards. Voters in Kansas City elected him mayor in 1916, a year before Jetta's death.

He and Isabella were Kehde's grandparents.

She would grow up in the Kansas City's Brookside area. She just happened to return to Lawrence when her first husband landed work at the University of Kansas. Then she moved away to study library sciences.

And now she's remarried and back in Lawrence, as if the legend of Quantrill's attack won't let her stray far. His raiders cut their trail just a few blocks from Pat Kehde's current home.

"Is it karma?" she asked. "I am certain there's some attraction. It's family."

# QUANTRILL HAS BEEN ON THE MOVE WELL OVER A CENTURY

By **DARRYL LEVINGS** ★ THE KANSAS CITY STAR

HIGGINSVILLE, Mo. | From the beginning, the state home for old rebels at Higginsville took in bushwhackers.

After all, the first superintendent, Mark Belt, had been one himself. Rode with Dave Pool before joining the regular Confederate army.

Always a bit blurry in Missouri's Civil War, the lines between bandits, bushwhackers, partisan rangers, rebel recruiters and actual CSA soldiers just got more so in the years when the old men with their long white beards told their stories.

By 1950, when they played taps for 108-year-old John Graves, Missouri's last rebel soldier, at least 14 one-time bushwhackers had slipped beneath the sod here. They lie with about 675 veterans, flanking the lovely "dying lion of the Confederacy" sculpture.

Which is our introduction to the tale of Quantrill's bones and why this quiet spot has held one of his graves — he has three, you know — for nearly 20 years.

"I find that he is a pretty big draw," said Kay Russell at what was once the Confederate Soldiers Home. "Almost constantly his grave is decorated by a flag or flowers."

In late 1864, William Clarke Quantrill, Frank James and others donned Union uniforms and slipped away, knowing things in Missouri would get hot once peace came. He came close to surviving the war but took a slug in the spine and died, at 27, on June 6, 1865, in Louisville, Ky.

There, Quantrill lay in an unmarked grave until his mother, Caroline Clarke Quantrill, decided in 1887 to bring him home to Dover, Ohio. She was helped by

William Walter Scott, who was researching a book on childhood buddy Willy C.

What followed? Skullduggery.

"So they dug him up and when Mr. Scott picked up the rib bones they kind of disintegrated, and so he only got the big bones," Russell said.

So bits still reside in Kentucky.

It's complicated, but Scott did not put the skull in the box with other bones. When he showed it to Mrs. Quantrill, she identified it as her son's by a particular tooth. (Science would find some of the bones not be Quantrill's, a sign his plot was recycled. Like we said, complicated.)

Back in Dover, did Scott bury the box in the Quantrill plot as he'd promised? No, he wrote to the Kansas Historical Society: "What would his skull be worth to your Society?"

The Topeka folks passed on that deal, yet ended up with Quantrill parts and a lock of his hair anyway.

When Scott died, his widow sold files and three arm bones to William E. Connelley, a Kansas historian publishing his own biography. Quantrill's soul, he wrote, was a "hideous, monstrous, misshapen thing."

Supposedly, Connelley tried to swap the bones for Jesse James' pistol but ended up donating them to the society, which after public harrumphing dis-

played them with two shin bones (given by Scott as a bonus enticement to buy the skull) and some Lawrence massacre relics.

The skull? Scott's son let a local fraternity have it for rituals. By 1972, the Dover Historical Society had it on display.

With new laws to make museums better respect Native American remains, the Quantrill bones, now in a tiny pine casket-like box, were stored far out of sight on a shelf at the Kansas archaeology lab.

Enter Robert L. Hawkins III.

"It came as a surprise to me that Quantrill's bones were in a box at the Kansas Historical Society," said the then Jefferson City lawyer and later Sons of Confederate Veterans national commander. He proposed a decent burial in the soil of Missouri.

Where better than Higginsville, amid all the other Yankee fighters?

Others, though, saw Dover as more appropriate.

"We were suggesting a very straightforward military disposal of the remains," Hawkins said. "There wasn't going to be anything particularly glorifying, but we did not want to see him ignored, either."

Agreement was not attained. So on Oct. 30, 1992, without

much ado, Quantrill's skull, in a white child's casket, went into the ground in Dover's Fourth Street Cemetery.

Hawkins was there, with perhaps a dozen others.

"They didn't hide it, it wasn't like they got it done in five minutes, and every body ran. It was very brief, but appropriate."

But Ohio is Yankee country. Missouri is not.

Six days earlier, just north of Higginsville, Hawkins and perhaps 800 people had witnessed the burial of the Kansas bones, bubbled-wrapped and snug in a glue-sealed Igloo cooler inside a regular-size, handmade oak casket.

A salute was fired by men wearing Confederate uniforms. A priest spoke, eulogies were offered, hymns were sung, including "What a Friend We Have in Jesus," a favorite of Jesse James.

As the casket was being lowered, a woman, supposedly a descendant of Dave Pool, one of Quantrill's band, rushed up and tossed in a black flag.

"I was less than pleased," recalled Hawkins, who now resides in Nashville. "We did not want those kinds of dramatic flourishes."

He earlier had nixed guerrilla re-enactors riding whooping out of nearby trees.

When things died down, sacks of cement were poured into the pit, a prophylactic against grave robbers.

The bones, at least, if not the soul, deserved the rest.

# MONUMENTS TO MAYHEM

Besides old battlefields, the places where the Civil War still lives most vividly are our cemeteries. With the 150th anniversary of the war, the old monuments become especially haunting.

In Forest Hill Cemetery, near Troost Avenue and 75th Street in Kansas City, is perhaps the region's biggest. The Confederate soldier atop it seems to gaze over Gen. Jo Shelby's grave toward the unattainable Westport. The most evocative monument is the dying lion of the Confederacy, erected at the graveyard of the old Confederate veterans home in Higginsville.

In other burial grounds, a sense of old grievance broods. At Osceola, burned to the ground in 1861 by Kansans under Sen. James Lane, rebel flags flutter at several old plots at the hilltop cemetery. Just west of Baxter Springs, Kan., a sad soldier of stone guards the bodies of Federal comrades chopped down in the high prairie grass by Quantrill's relentless band.

Nearly 100 Kansas and Wisconsin soldiers were moved to this little National Cemetery, including all the musicians of Maj. Gen. James Blunt's band, who were shot and burned in their wagon with their instruments by angry guerrillas.

Waverly, Mo., erected an equestrian statue honoring favorite son Joseph Orville "Jo" Shelby, who did well in the hemp business in the little Missouri River town, but even better as a cavalry raider in the war.

At Keytesville, Mo., Gov. Sterling Price's home before the war, the town square proudly displays a likeness of the Confederate major general, whom Jefferson Davis called the vainest man he ever met.

The centerpiece among the rebel graves at Higginsville, Mo., is a copy of the famous "Lion of Lucerne," the Swiss original called by Mark Twain "the most mournful and moving piece of stone in the world."

They called lone, charred chimneys "Jennison tombstones" after the jayhawking Kansas colonel. Now a new one stands in Harrisonville as a memorial to the "Burnt District's" torched homesteads.

George Gaston's monument in Forest Hill Cemetery booms the pride of an artillerist. An officer in the Bavarian army, he immigrated in 1861 to New York and donned a captain's new blue uniform.

Lt. Gen. Ulysses S. Grant's impressive nine-foot statue, including his slouch hat, was erected by admirers after his death to greet those coming into Fort Leavenworth's old main gate.

At Oak Hill Cemetery in Lawrence, most of the men and boys gunned down or burned to death in the Quantrill raid of August 1863 were reburied not far from a somber 1895 monument to them.

# FACES OF WAR

As the war progressed, both North and South tended to look at the Trans-MIssissippi as a second-rarte theater of war to be staffed by second-rate generals.

While some officers did fulfill this pigeonholing, others showed tactical brilliance and amazing fighting abilities. Professional soldiers were here, but also hatters, hemp kings, doctors and engineers, farm boys and governors in civilian life.

## UNION LEADERSHIP AT THE BATTLE OF WESTPORT

**Maj. Gen. Samuel Curtis** won at Pea Ridge and Westport but lost his son, murdered after surrendering to guerrillas at Baxter Springs.

**Maj. Gen. James G. Blunt,** a fierce fighter but banished to Indian chasing after the Baxter Springs debacle, saw his career saved at Westport.

**Maj. Gen. Alfred Pleasonton,** once cavalry chief in the East before he was exiled to Missouri, was nearly as aggressive as he was abrasive.

**Col. John Philips,** later a lawyer for Frank James in his murder trial, led Missourians across Byram's Ford, then to a smashing Mine Creek win.

**Gen. John McNeil,** "Butcher of Palmyra," lost nerve at south crossing on Blue River, letting Price's army escape being bagged after Westport fight.

## CONFEDERATE LEADERSHIP AT THE BATTLE OF WESTPORT

**Maj. Gen. Sterling Price, "Ol' Pap,"** took the last shot in the fall of 1864 to regain Missouri, only to see the army crushed in Mine Creek, Kan.

**Maj. Gen. John Marmaduke** survived Shiloh but got pushed off Byram's Ford and then captured in the Mine Creek rout.

**Gen. Jo Shelby,** a hemp magnate who led wiry veterans of the Iron Brigade, was the best cavalry commander this side of Mississippi.

**Gen. John Clark** studied law with Col. John Philips, then fought him tooth and nail at Byram's Ford before being pushed south in retreat.

**Gen. M. Jeff Thompson** got off a Union prison boat in Charleston, S.C., just in time to join Price and lead the Iron Brigade at Brush Creek.

# FACES OF WAR

## OTHER PLAYERS IN THE LONG-RUNNING DRAMA OF THE BORDER

**Brig. Gen. Thomas Ewing (left) issued Order No. 11 in 1863, emptying Missouri counties after William Quantrill (right) killed up to 200 men and boys in Lawrence. Ewing went on to Washington to defend Lincoln assassination plotters, Quantrill to Kentucky and a bullet in the spine.**

**Maj. A.V.E. Johnson (right), a schoolteacher and would-be-avenger of the Centralia massacre, promptly led his men into a worse slaughter just outside town. The story goes that he got his bullet in the head from Jesse James (left), a boy of 17 who was one of Anderson's best men.**

**William "Bloody Bill" Anderson lived up to his name by scalping victims, including unarmed soldiers on a Centralia train.**

**Col. Charles "Doc" Jennison's harsh jayhawking ways terrified Missourians but got him kicked out of the Army in the end.**

**Margaret Watts Hays lost her husband, Upton, to the war, her home to jayhawkers, her Westport farm to Order No. 11.**

**Lt. William Mathews, once an Underground Railroad engineer, became one of the nation's first black officers leading his race to war.**

COURTESY OF WILSON'S CREEK NATIONAL BATTLEFIELD, NATIONAL PARK SERVICE, FOR MOST PHOTOGRAPHS DISPLAYED; OF THE STATE HISTORICAL SOCIETY IN COLUMBIA FOR IMAGES OF JOHNSON AND ANDERSON; OF THE KANSAS HISTORICAL SOCIETY IN TOPEKA FOR MATHEWS; OF WATTSHAYSLETTERS. COM FOR HAYS

**Fort Leavenworth's** Frontier Army Museum tells much about its role in the conquering of the West, but is thin on the Civil War, considering its headquarters role for jayhawkers. Lots of cannon, a fine statue of Ulysses S. Grant, though. Don't miss the chapel.

**Lecompton** is the place for pre-statehood history, with its Constitutional Hall just nouth of I-70 between Lawrence and Topeka.

**Topeka's** west end has the State Historical Society's fine museum, with significant "Bleeding Kansas" and Civil War artifacts. Follow I-70 west to the Wanamaker Road exit, go north to the traffic circle. Swing off to the west on S.W. 6th Avenue and follow it literally to the end of the road. It's down there.

At **Lawrence**, you'll still find a smattering of remnants of a massacre. Grab the Convention & Visitors Bureau's self-guided tour brochure. One can step though Oak Hill Cemetery, where many victims of the 1863 onslaught from Quantrill's raiders were re-interred. The only downtown structure that survived is the House Building, 729 Massachusetts St.

**Harrisonville**, on U.S. 71, has one of the newer Civil War stops — the Burnt District Monument on the grounds of the Cass County Justice Center just off Missouri 2.

**Butler's** courthouse square is guarded by the statue of a black Union infantryman. West of town, the 1st Kansas Colored Infantry, many of the men former slaves, battled rebels on Oct. 29, 1862, a first for the Civil War and the country.

At **Osawatomie**, down U.S. 169, is the John Brown Museum State Historic Site.

**Fort Scott**, a major supply depot for Federal forts and campaigns to the south, looks very much like it did during the Civil War.

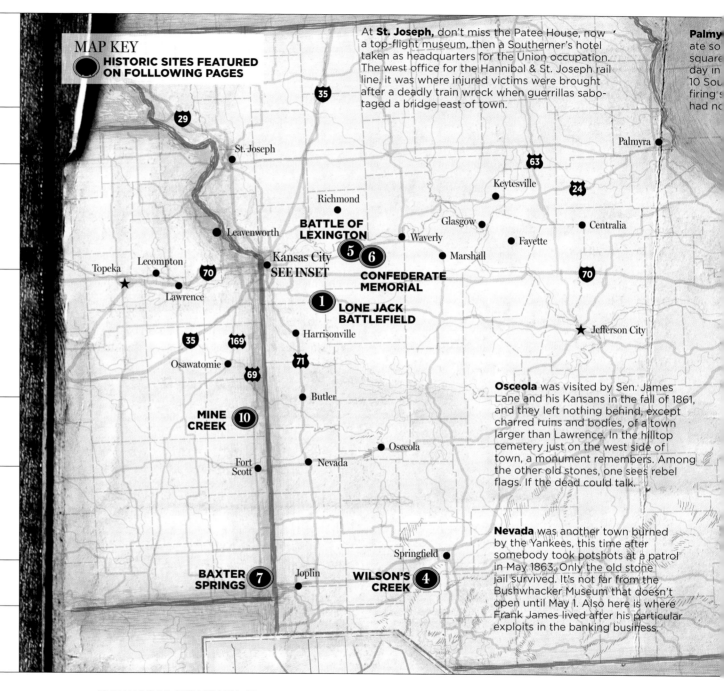

At **St. Joseph,** don't miss the Patee House, now a top-flight museum, then a Southerner's hotel taken as headquarters for the Union occupation. The west office for the Hannibal & St. Joseph rail line, it was where injured victims were brought after a deadly train wreck when guerrillas sabotaged a bridge east of town.

**Palmy** ate so square day in '10 Sou firing' had n

MAP KEY
● HISTORIC SITES FEATURED ON FOLLLOWING PAGES

**Osceola** was visited by Sen. James Lane and his Kansans in the fall of 1861, and they left nothing behind, except charred ruins and bodies, of a town larger than Lawrence. In the hilltop cemetery just on the west side of town, a monument remembers. Among the other old stones, one sees rebel flags. If the dead could talk.

**Nevada** was another town burned by the Yankees, this time after somebody took potshots at a patrol in May 1863. Only the old stone jail survived. It's not far from the Bushwhacker Museum that doesn't open until May 1. Also here is where Frank James lived after his particular exploits in the banking business.

stone Confeder-
the courthouse
emplate the
en Federals put
en in front of a
r a murder they
itted.

**At Richmond** is the grave of Bloody Bill Anderson, where the guerrilla killer was dumped into a long-unmarked hole. It's in the old Mormon or Pioneer Cemetery, waaaay over in a corner far from the decent folk.

**Waverly,** pre-war home of Confederate Gen. Jo Shelby, has put up a sculpture depicting him. The town is holding a different kind of re-enactment June 25, staging the wedding between their famous son and his wife.

**Keytesville** was the pre-war home of Sterling Price, so here is a fine statue of the governor/general. Also on Bridge Street is a Price museum, full of great stories, and generally open Monday through Friday.

**Glasgow** suffered when Price's hungry, ill-armed army came looking for supplies in '64. That's why Gens. Jo Shelby and John Clark defeated a Union force in a sharp little battle here on Oct. 15, 1864, involving house-to-house fighting, a burning steamboat and bushwhacker visits. Good information down at the waterfront.

**Marshall** is where Shelby's famous 1863 cavalry raid up from Arkansas nearly came to an end, but in the battle he slipped the trap by dividing his outnumbered force. Marker at "battle" gazebo in Indian Foothills Park.

**At Jefferson City**, the state is redoing a south wall of the museum for the war's anniversary. It will be ready May 1. Don't miss the two N.C. Wyeth murals of the Wilson's Creek and Westport battles upstairs. Not particularly strong on accuracy, they are glorious. (The Westport painting can be found on the cover of this section.)

**Centralia,** on Sept. 27, 1864, was a bad place for a Union solider to be. Bloody Bill Anderson's bushwhackers took about two dozen furloughed soldiers from a captured train and slaughtered them in their underwear. When Missouri mounted infantry arrived, most ended up with bullets in their heads as well. An information tablet is at the corner of the town park; to walk the battlefield just to the southeast, follow signs.

ouis, a new Mis-
vil War Museum
n this summer
estored Post
ge Building at
Jefferson Bar-
south St. Louis.
allation was one
argest military
s during the war,
000 Civil War
st in the National
ry there.

Reminders of the violence that first flared in our backyard can still be seen nearby. Here's a guide to some important sites with a comfortable days' drive of Kansas City.

# CIVIL WAR TOUR

By DARRYL LEVINGS & NEIL NAKAHODO ★ THE KANSAS CITY STAR

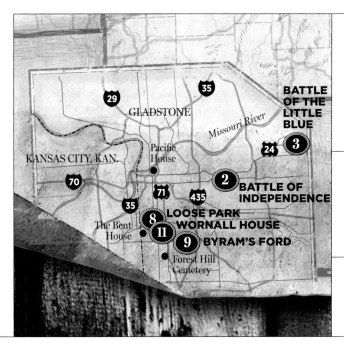

In **Forest Hill Cemetery** on Troost Avenue a little north of Gregory Boulevard, a Confederate soldier stands atop a tall column and looks a little wistfully toward Westport. Shelby is buried here as are other rebels and and guerrillas. Look on next hill to the northeast for the cannon tombstone of New York artillery Capt. Geroge Gaston.

**The Pacific House**, on Delaware in Kansas City's City Market area, was a hotel and Federal headquarters for Gen. Thomas Ewing, the fellow who signed Order No. 11 after the deadly Lawrence raid.

**The Bent House**, peeking from behind the Seth Ward House, a private residence, was on Shelby's left flank, turned by Federal cannon popping out of the timber.

## LONE JACK BATTLEFIELD

The Jackson County countryside swarmed with rebel recruits and guer-rillas in summer of '62. Perhaps 3,000 were camped around this hamlet when 700 Missouri militia cavalrymen showed up late on Aug. 15. The next morning, some of the fiercest fighting in the state erupted as the ill-armed rebels tried a surprise attack.

**WHAT TO SEE; HOW TO FIND IT:**

A small battlefield park holds a little cemetery; next door is a museum that explains the battle well. Follow U.S. 50 east of Lee's Summit; turn right on Bynum Road (Route E).

## FIRST BATTLE OF INDEPENDENCE

It's a two-for-one deal for the old county seat, which on 1862 saw rebels rush in for a pre-dawn surprise attack on sol-diers camped west of Pleasant Street and the Federal headquarters. Some soldiers ran for it, others fought back hard from a stone wall. This fight also saw William C. Quantrill's contingent capture the city jail. Two years later, Maj. Gen. Sterling Price's army pushed the Federals west through Independence, then had the same thing happen to them the next day as hard-charging Federal brigades from Jefferson City arrived.

**WHAT TO SEE; HOW TO FIND IT:**

Best bet is the old city jail on Main Street. Ask them about James Knowles, the city marshal who was inside a cell when bushwhackers visited. A block south is the courthouse, which has a useful battle tablet on south side. From the porch at the Bingham-Waggoner Home, restored to post-Civil-War glory at 313 W. Pacific Ave., ladies admired the gallantry of the 1864 struggle to the west over Gen. William Cabell's cannon. George Caleb Bingham painted his fa-mous "Order No. 11" in a log cabin, long gone, on the front yard.

## BATTLE OF THE LITTLE BLUE

On Oct. 21, 1864, Price's army pushing along the Lexington Road slammed into a brigade of tough Kansas cavalry. Maj. Gen. James Blunt brought reinforce-ments, but overwhelming numbers

forced him back past Independence to the next river, the Big Blue.

**WHAT TO SEE; HOW TO FIND IT:**

Travel east on U.S. 24 until the highway begins to dip toward the river. Take the last right and follow the road to the river parkway. Informative markers are there, as well as at the Blue Mills Road. Just a mile down that road on the right is the Lawson Moore house, a private residence. Vacated by Order No. 11, the house held the wounded. Those who didn't make it were buried in the yard. Bushwhacker leader George Todd literally got it in the neck near here, many believe by a 2nd Colorado cavalry carbine. His incorrect grave stone is in Woodlawn Cemetery, 701 Noland Road, a pistol shot from an old marker for Colorado men, some ambushed by Todd

in earlier months.

## WILSON'S CREEK NATIONAL BATTLEFIELD

This is the premier battlefield in Mis-souri, hundreds of acres of pristine hills and fields, just about as those 16,000 sol-diers here would have seen them on that awful day, Aug. 10, 1861. Gen. Nathaniel Lyon — facing a rebel force twice as large as his own — attacked early in the morning, beginning six hours of fighting across the slopes of Bloody Hill. More than 500 men died, including Lyon, the first Union general to be killed.

**WHAT TO SEE; HOW TO FIND IT:**

One can drive a 5-mile loop that has interpretive stops, some with audio,

at key points. This costs $10 a car. The visitors center has an array of Civil War portraits, but the park's real treasure trove is across the road at the must-see museum collection of Dr. Thomas Sweeney. A re-enactment will be held here on the anniversary of the battle. Approach the site from the west side of Springfield; taking Interstate 44 until Exit 70, traveling south first on Missouri MM, then ZZ.

 **5**

## BATTLE OF LEXINGTON

The richest Civil War location in the Kansas City area is this river town about an hour from Kansas City. Its streets flaunt antebellum homes; its old courthouse sports a cannon ball in its

east column, a leftover from when Price came to town Sept. 13, 1861.

**WHAT TO SEE; HOW TO FIND IT:**

We recommend a long Sunday here. The ground clearly shows where U.S. Maj. James Mulligan had his trenches dug for the siege. Also the scars of the battle are all over the east wall of the Anderson House. It's behind the excellent state museum where not just the climatic Sept. 20 "Battle of the Hemp Bales" is explained, but also antebellum life before. Also, black powder smoke will roll just east of town on Sept. 17-18 as thousands show up for what organizers hope will be Missouri's largest re-enactment. U.S. 24 east is the most direct route; taking I-70 means exiting at Missouri 13.

 **6**

## CONFEDERATE MEMORIAL STATE HISTORIC SITE

Missouri's old soldiers home sheltered 1,600 Confederate veterans and their families for nearly 60 years. The last died in 1950, joining comrades in the cemetery guarded by the dying lion of the Confederacy.

**WHAT TO SEE; HOW TO FIND IT:**

Note the stone of Richard Collins, artillery captain to the "Iron Brigade." It says simply: "One of Shelby's Men." To a Southerner, enough said. Now part of a state park, the cemetery can be found at Missouri 20 and Missouri 213 just north of Higginsville.

 **7**

## BAXTER SPRINGS, KAN.

Two months after Quantrill and his men burned Lawrence and killed maybe 200 mostly unarmed men and boys, they massacred about 90 Union soldiers here. About 400 Texas-bound bushwhackers couldn't crack the little Fort Blair at the springs, but ripped into Maj. Gen. James Blunt's escort of 150 cavalry troopers and some wagons, one carrying his band. No one was allowed to surrender, even the musicians. Sgt. Jack Splane was found still breathing despite wounds in

the head, chest, guts, arm and leg. Last thing he heard? A bushwhacker saying: "Tell old God that the last man you saw on Earth was Quantrill."

**WHAT TO SEE; HOW TO FIND IT:**

A rough outline of Fort Blair is in a city park on the north side of town. A half block away at 740 East Avenue is the Baxter Springs Heritage Center and Museum with a good amount of Civil War material. A few markers off U.S. 69 show where Blunt's men scattered, but the "don't miss" item is the cemetery on U.S. 166 west of town. The central monument naming those who died Oct. 9, 1863, is impressive.

 **8**

## LOOSE PARK

On the unquiet Sunday of Oct. 23, 1864, Gen. Jo Shelby's division fought back and forth all morning over fields and fences with Blunt's cavalry brigades here. A final Federal push across Brush Creek about noon — about the same time that Maj. Gen. Alfred Pleasonton's

**WHAT TO SEE; HOW TO FIND IT:** At the double-towered Battle of Westport Visitor Center Museum (open 1-5 p.m. Thursday through Saturday) by the west entrance to Swope Park, the struggle is well explained. A cannon near the Water Department office just north of 63rd shows Marmaduke's position. A marker on Manchester Trafficway is just east of the railroad tracks (watch carefully). One can get to the ford, as well.

This is an excellent site, with a walking tour of the battlefield down to the ford where Price's wagons had bottlenecked his retreat. The state operates a top-flight museum here as well. Take U.S. 69 south and turn left on Kansas 52. It's easily seen on the left side of the road.

forces showed up on his flank and in his rear and convinced Shelby that it was time to cut his way out. He barely made it.

**WHAT TO SEE; HOW TO FIND IT:**
Some wanted this land for a "Gettysburg of the West," but Mrs. Jacob Loose purchased it for a park. Now, a Parrott gun replica and good informational tablets about the battle are at the park's south end, close to 55th Street. Area streets are sprinkled with markers, although some are a bit inaccurate, such as the one just south of the duck pond. It says Arkansas Col. James McGee was killed during a charge. He was not. His name also was spelled "McGehee."

### BYRAM'S FORD

The Battle of Westport of Oct. 23 was fought on two fronts. About three miles to the southeast was Byram's Ford across the Big Blue. The Federals had failed to keep the rebels from crossing here the day before. But the more numerous Confederates made a better effort trying to hold off Pleasonton's cavalry. Hot lead and iron erupting from the high ground left many Union dead here. Outgunned and out of ammo, Maj. Gen. John S. Marmaduke retreated south along the Harrisonville Road (Prospect Avenue), leaving exposed the rebel soldiers falling back from Westport.

### MINE CREEK

Two days after the battle near Westport, Confederate forces found themselves pinned against this little stream. In the largest cavalry action west of the Mississippi, two bold brigades of Union cavalry barreled into two rebel divisions, shattering them. In the rout, the Yankees captured hundreds, including two generals and all the reb guns. One reason for the very lop-sided casualty lists of Oct. 25? Many of the ragged rebel soldiers were wearing parts of stolen Union uniforms to keep warm. They were shot for it.

**WHAT TO SEE; HOW TO FIND IT:**

### WORNALL HOUSE

What we now know as Wornall Road south of the Plaza was the Fort Scott Road. Some called it "Bloody Lane." In June '63, an ambush by George Todd left 13 dead 9th Kansas Cavalry troopers. In the '64 engagement, both armies surged up and down the road, cannon blasting down its muddy path. The house that gives the street its name was used as a hospital. Notorious jayhawker Col. Charles "Doc" Jennison used it as a headquarters in late '61 or early '62.

**WHAT TO SEE: HOW TO FIND IT:**
The 1858 Greek Revival home at 6115 Wornall Road operates as a fine museum showing the lifestyle of the Civil War era.

# A GLOSSARY OF LOCAL TERMS FROM THE CIVIL WAR ERA

**The following is a glossary of terms that one might encounter during the observation of the 150th anniversary of the American Civil War.**

**Bushwhackers:** In the Kansas City area, bushwhacker meant any violent Southern guerrilla and/or bandit. Federal officials applied the term as well to men commissioned as partisan rangers and roving Confederate recruiters. A verb as well as a noun, bushwhacking was not exclusive to the Kansas/Missouri region. In other sectors of the war, one finds references to Union bushwhacking.

**Jayhawkers:** The 7th Kansas Cavalry under Col. Charles "Doc" Jennison and Lt. Col. Daniel Anthony were the "official" jayhawkers. In late 1861 and early 1862, they burned towns in Missouri and plundered widely, causing federal district commanders to complain that more rebels were being created than killed by the regiment. As a result, it was sent across the Mississippi River away from the border area. Another verb/noun: Jayhawking was an activity that today would get you in prison. Not exclusive to Kansans, as some Missouri Union men joined Kansas units, and Southerners living within 50 miles of the border often blamed any federal atrocity, even if committed by a state militia, on "jayhawkers." Again, not exclusive to the area: In Louisiana, men with Union sympathies were referred to as jayhawkers.

**Missouri State Guard:** In the early weeks of the war, when Missouri was trying for armed neutrality, this force was assembled to protect against invasion. It and its commanders were decidedly pro-Southern, although not part of the Confederate army until after Missouri seceded in October 1861. In the August Battle of Wilson's Creek, for example, Gen. Sterling Price's State Guard teamed with Gen. Ben McCulloch's Confederate regiments to defeat the Federals. Not to be confused with the Home Guard, an ineffective local militia raised among Union supporters in several towns.

**Missouri militias:** No other state had what was organized here — first the Missouri State Militia, then also the Enrolled Missouri Militia. The tough Missouri State Militia cavalry regiments were raised to fight guerrillas. Equipped and paid for by Washington, they were designed strictly for action in this state. The Enrolled Missouri Militia was a much larger organization; in effect, every able-bodied man in Missouri was supposed to sign up. This order, however, meant a lot of Southerners who didn't want to fight for the Union or against kin slipped away into the bush or down into Arkansas to enlist in the Confederate army. The fighting quality of Enrolled Missouri Militias, who had no uniforms, varied greatly from county to county. Later in the war, some Provisional Enrolled Missouri Militias were created from the better fighters among Enrolled Missouri Militias.

**Red Legs:** A somewhat different species than jayhawkers, although with some interchangeable characters and activities. Neither Jennison nor acolyte Capt. George Hoyt wished to leave their border activities behind, so they resigned from the 7th. Hoyt enlisted a band of hard men who are described variously and not exclusively as a deadly paramilitary force, provost-marshal detectives and horse thieves extraordinaire. They got their names from their distinctive leggings, red-dyed sheepskin or yarn. Jennison, who went into livestock and freighting, is believed to have been the conduit of stolen Missouri goods to Colorado.

# MAPPING THE BATTLES

## MAJOR EVENTS IN MISSOURI AND KANSAS

By DARRYL LEVINGS & DAVE EAMES ★ THE KANSAS CITY STAR

### Union

➡ Line

➡ Advance

⭢ Retreat

### Confederates

➡ Line

➡ Advance

⭢ Retreat

SOURCES FOR THE FOLLOWING BATTLE MAPS: MINE CREEK BATTLEFIELD FOUNDATION, NATIONAL PARK SERVICE, LONE JACK HISTORICAL SOCIETY AND THE INDEPENDENCE TOURISM DEPARTMENT

## 1861

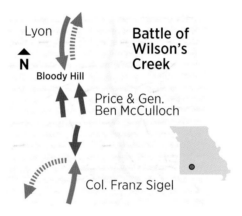

Maj. Gen. Sterling Price's Missouri State Guard and Arkansas troops were eating breakfast south of the Springfield when Union forces under Gen. Nathanial Lyon split his smaller force and attacked. Lyon paid with his life.

Price's little army then beseiged Lexington, forcing its surrender before falling back to Arkansas.

# 1862

Price's attempt to reinvade Missouri was foiled at Pea Ridge in Arkansas, but Federal forces took lickings locally. Rebels, including William Quantrill, made a pre-breakfast raid into Independence and forced Union surrender.

**First Battle of Independence**

Pleasant St.

Lt. Col. James Buel headquarters besieged

Jail

Maple St.

■ Courthouse

Walnut St.

■ Sleeping camp attacked

N

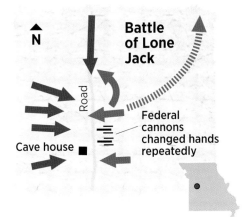

N

**Battle of Lone Jack**

Road

Cave house

Federal cannons changed hands repeatedly

Days later, pursuing Federals were nearly overwhelmed in a particularly bloody affair at Lone Jack in southeast Jackson County.

# 1863

The year is remembered most for when Quantrill's raiders rode deep into Kansas to leave the streets of Lawrence filled with dead

N

Kansas River

6th St.

**Downtown**

9th St.

Mass. St.

Mt. Oread

**Raid on Lawrence**

Oregon Trail

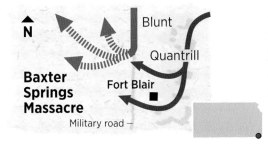

N

Blunt

Quantrill

**Baxter Springs Massacre**

Fort Blair

Military road —

A second massacre came when Quantrill caught Maj. Gen. James Blunt and his escort after attacking Fort Blair at Baxter Springs, Kan.

# THE BATTLES OF 1864

## MAJOR EVENTS IN MISSOURI AND KANSAS

By DARRYL LEVINGS & DAVE EAMES ★ THE KANSAS CITY STAR

By the autumn 1864 effort to invade Missouri, the flame of rebellion was growing dim. Richmond was under siege, Atlanta captured, the Mississippi River a Federal wedge between Southern sections. Maj. Gen. Sterling Price's plan was to capture St. Louis and embarrass Abraham Lincoln at election time, draw away Union forces crushing the Confederates in the east, attract a host of new recruits and grab badly needed supplies.

Price gave up on his goal of capturing St. Louis. His army suffered many casualties attacking Fort Davidson at Pilot Knob, which discouraged him from trying to storm Jefferson City. His march turned toward Kansas as Federal forces assembled to trap and crush him.

# BATTLE OF THE LITTLE BLUE
## OCT. 21, 1864

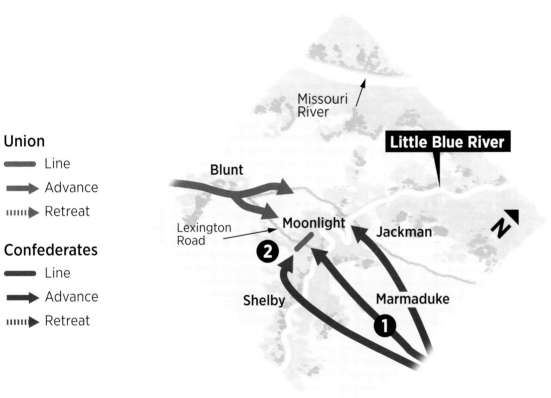

**Union**

➤ Line

➤ Advance

▷ Retreat

**Confederates**

➤ Line

➤ Advance

▷ Retreat

The aggressive Maj. Gen. James Blunt believed the topography at the Little Blue River, east of Independence, favored his defense. Despite his superior firepower, however, he was badly outnumbered.

**1** Maj. Gen. John Marmaduke's division first came down the Lexington Road and hit Col. Thomas Moonlight's tough 11th Kansas Cavalry. Blunt brought up two more brigades.

**2** Gen. Jo Shelby's brigades under Gen. M. Jeff Thompson and Col. Sidney Jackman also crossed the river and began lapping around the lines of Blunt, who grudgingly retreated through Independence.

# BATTLE OF THE BIG BLUE
## OCT. 22, 1864

**Maj Gen. Samuel Curtis deployed Blunt's cavalry and thousands of Kansas militiamen along the Blue River, trying to hold Price until Maj. Gen. Alfred Pleasonton could bring up his cavalry and smash the Confederate rear.**

**3** Price feinted at a northern crossing, then Shelby's division pushed Col. Charles "Doc" Jennison's 15th Kansas Cavalry off Byram's Ford.

**4** Jackman's rebels smash Topeka's 2nd Kansas militia regiment at Mockbee Farm, leaving many dead on both sides.

**5** Jennison and Moonlight fall back to Kansas line. Pleasonton pushes Price rear guard through Independence.

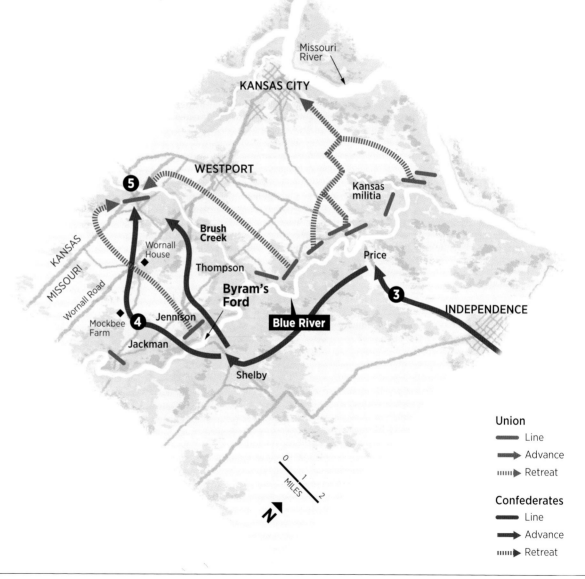

# BATTLE OF WESTPORT
## OCT. 23, 1864

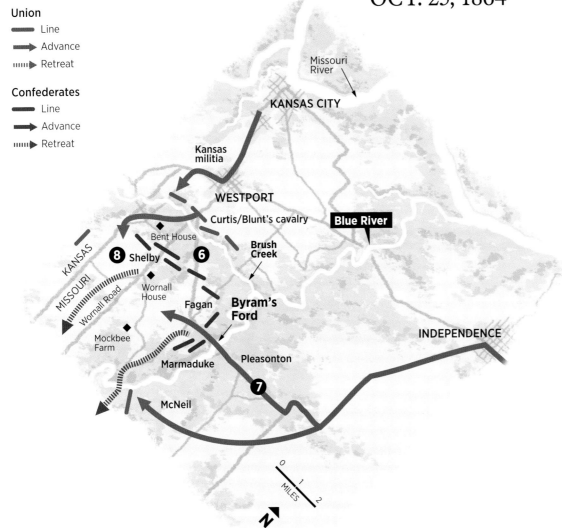

**Union**
Line
Advance
Retreat

**Confederates**
Line
Advance
Retreat

Missouri River
KANSAS CITY
Kansas militia
WESTPORT
Curtis/Blunt's cavalry
Blue River
KANSAS
MISSOURI
Bent House
Brush Creek
Wornall Road
Wornall House
Fagan
Byram's Ford
Mockbee Farm
Marmaduke
Pleasonton
McNeil
INDEPENDENCE

8 Shelby
6
7

0 1 2 MILES

N

**On this Sunday, Price was in a box, but he hoped to whip the Federals under Curtis and Blunt in Westport, then turn on Pleasonton, who now was at Byram's Ford.**

**6** Blunt and Shelby collide south of Brush Creek; Blunt is forced to north side of creek.

**7** Pleasonton pushes across Byram's Ford into hail of fire from Marmaduke's division on high ground. Outgunned and low on ammunition, the Confederates withdraw, leading Shelby to weaken his line near Brush Creek. Curtis brings up guns near Bent House to strike Thompson's left flank.

**8** Around noon, Blunt, now reinforced and with more cannon, attack Shelby, who realizes Pleasonton's brigades are in his rear. Some of Shelby's regiments are scattered; others fight holding actions as Price's column retreats. Gen. John McNeil fails to block Blue.pendence.

# BATTLE OF MINE CREEK
## OCT. 25, 1864

**The Federal pursuit is helped by the slowness of Price's long wagon train. With their backs to Mine Creek, about 40 miles south of Johnson County, Kan., the divisions of Marmaduke and Fagan turn and face two brigades of Federal horsemen under Col. John Philips and Lt. Col. George Benteen.**

**9** Iowa cavalry fishhook around Marmaduke's right flank, and his force panics. Generals John Marmaduke and William Cabell are captured along with hundreds of other rebel soldiers. Many are executed on the spot for wearing Union overcoats.

**10** Shelby fights rear guard actions, Price burns many of his wagons, and the retreat continues. They fight one last battle at Newtonia, a draw, before a miserable retreat to Texas.

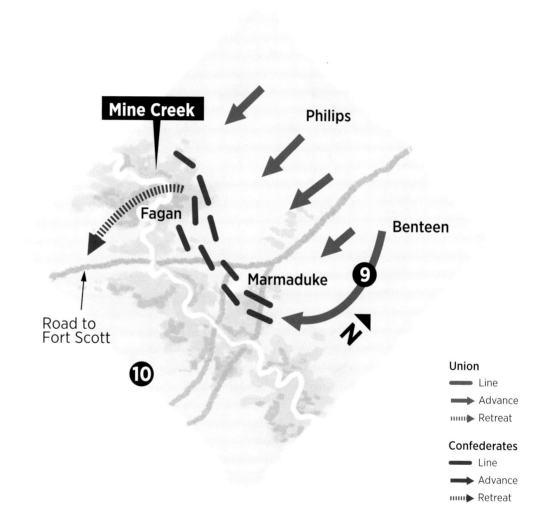

Mine Creek

Philips

Fagan

Benteen

Marmaduke

**9**

Road to Fort Scott

**10**

N

**Union**
— Line
➡ Advance
⟩ Retreat

**Confederates**
— Line
➡ Advance
⟩ Retreat

# Part 2

# Freedom's distant cry

As the nation marks the Civil War's sesquicentennial, many African-Americans still struggle to reconcile the painful legacy of slavery with valor of 200,000 black soldiers who fought to end it.

By MARÁ ROSE WILLIAMS & GLENN E. RICE ★ THE KANSAS CITY STAR

BUTLER, Mo. | The wind-whipped field looks no different from millions of others. Even as a field of battle, it is hardly distinguishable from thousands.

But these grassy acres west of town are hallowed.

Here, in October 1862, black men — escaped slaves and freedmen both — fought rebels in a bloody hand-to-hand skirmish as an American unit for the first time.

"Like tigers," noted one Southern man who tangled with them here at Island Mound.

Willadine Johnson and her cousins had known nothing about the bravery of these African-American defenders of their country or how this moment made an early, indelible imprint in

Jimmy Johnson often portrays his great-grandfather, who fought in 1862 at the Battle of Island Mound in Bates County, Mo., the first combat engagement of African-American soldiers in the Civil War. Johnson posed at the Bates County Museum outside Butler, where the battle is depicted in a mural by artist Richard Carter. | KEITH MYERS, THE KANSAS CITY STAR

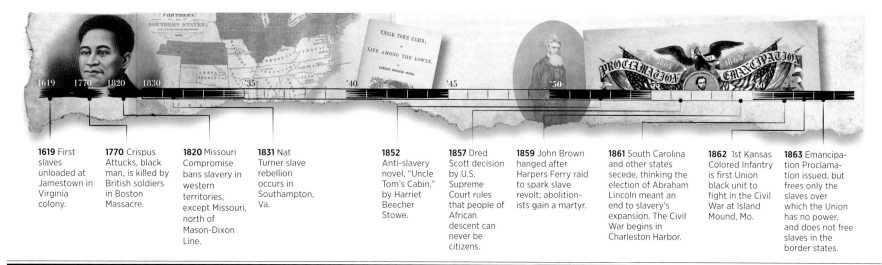

**1619** First slaves unloaded at Jamestown in Virginia colony.

**1770** Crispus Attucks, black man, is killed by British soldiers in Boston Massacre.

**1820** Missouri Compromise bans slavery in western territories, except Missouri, north of Mason-Dixon Line.

**1831** Nat Turner slave rebellion occurs in Southampton, Va.

**1852** Anti-slavery novel, "Uncle Tom's Cabin," by Harriet Beecher Stowe.

**1857** Dred Scott decision by U.S. Supreme Court rules that people of African descent can never be citizens.

**1859** John Brown hanged after Harpers Ferry raid to spark slave revolt; abolitionists gain a martyr.

**1861** South Carolina and other states secede, thinking the election of Abraham Lincoln meant an end to slavery's expansion. The Civil War begins in Charleston Harbor.

**1862** 1st Kansas Colored Infantry is first Union black unit to fight in the Civil War at Island Mound, Mo.

**1863** Emancipation Proclamation issued, but frees only the slaves over which the Union has no power, and does not free slaves in the border states.

---

the uneven, bitterly long and sometimes bloody path to equality to be trod by their descendants.

But when they began looking into their family history, they found it — in the form of a bronze statue of a Union infantryman — staring back at them on the lawn of the Bates County Courthouse.

Civil War soldiers are fixtures on courthouse squares across half of America, but this one, erected in 2008 about 50 miles south of Kansas City, was of an African-American.

"We just filled up with this pride." White America did not think black men could fight, Johnson said, "But they did. They fought valiantly and gallantly. They did not give up."

Cpl. Rufus Vann, her great-great-grandfather, marched into Bates County with the 1st Kansas Colored Volunteer Infantry Regiment, she said. He was among the 200,000 black men who would fill out the ranks of the Union army.

Like 40,000 of his comrades of color, Vann did not survive. His 1865 death in Little Rock, not from bullets but from disease, was typical for the Civil War soldier.

Impressive numbers, yet, for many African-Americans, it is difficult to embrace the 150th anniversary of the war.

While white Civil War enthusiasts don uniforms — with a decided preference in Missouri for gray — and women slip into silk hoop skirts for balls, few African-Americans care to dress up as slaves.

"A dozen or so here and there" will participate as soldiers in battle re-enactments, said Hari Jones, curator of the African-American Civil War Memorial and Museum.

Jones blames "propaganda" that twisted the history of the black experience. Much Civil War literature, illustration and film, from "The Birth of a Nation" to "Gone With the Wind," depicted African-Americans as pathetic, simpleminded, subservient and depen-

dent.

"I'm sure that if they really knew the history of how African-Americans fought for their freedom, at Island Mound, Fort Wagner, at Honey Springs in Indian Territory, the Battle of Vicksburg and so many others, they would feel differently about their African-American history," Jones said.

"For African-Americans not to celebrate the anniversary of the Civil War would be like Americans not to pop firecrackers on the Fourth of July."

To that, the Rev. David A. Gilmore, pastor of Centennial United Methodist Church in Kansas City, replies that he knows of black Americans, "who, not only do they not celebrate the Civil War, but they don't even celebrate the Fourth of July or call it Independence Day, because on that day in 1776 black people were still slaves."

"It is easy to celebrate the end of something if you have been delivered from it," he said. "But if you ci-

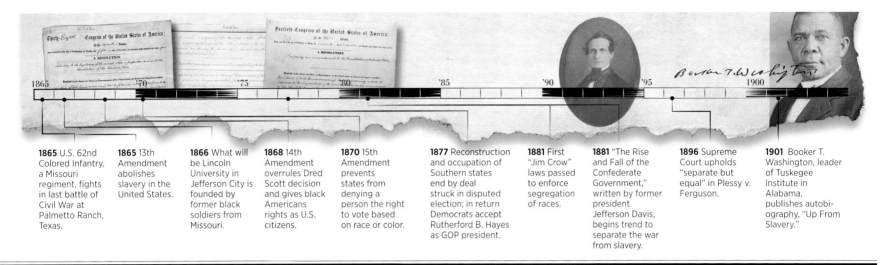

**1865** U.S. 62nd Colored Infantry, a Missouri regiment, fights in last battle of Civil War at Palmetto Ranch, Texas.

**1865** 13th Amendment abolishes slavery in the United States.

**1866** What will be Lincoln University in Jefferson City is founded by former black soldiers from Missouri.

**1868** 14th Amendment overrules Dred Scott decision and gives black Americans rights as U.S. citizens.

**1870** 15th Amendment prevents states from denying a person the right to vote based on race or color.

**1877** Reconstruction and occupation of Southern states end by deal struck in disputed election; in return Democrats accept Rutherford B. Hayes as GOP president.

**1881** First "Jim Crow" laws passed to enforce segregation of races.

**1881** "The Rise and Fall of the Confederate Government," written by former president Jefferson Davis, begins trend to separate the war from slavery.

**1896** Supreme Court upholds "separate but equal" in Plessy v. Ferguson.

**1901** Booker T. Washington, leader of Tuskegee Institute in Alabama, publishes autobiography, "Up From Slavery."

---

ther consciously or subconsciously feel you are still caught in the throes of this thing, it is hard. As a people, we have not been delivered."

★ ★ ★

Shortly after the war began, a Virginia slave named Harry Jarvis slipped off to Fort Monroe, held by Union Gen. Benjamin Butler. He asked to enlist, but Butler said no, that "it wasn't a black man's war."

"I told him it would be a black man's war before they got through," recounted Jarvis, who was made a laborer as "contraband of war."

Although black men had fought as individuals in the Revolution and in the War of 1812, a 1792 law barred them from the U.S. Army.

Even in spring 1861, when Washington looked as if it would fall before any Northern forces reached it, 300 of the capital's free black community gathered

for its defense. The War Department replied that it had "no intention ... to call into the service of the Government any colored soldiers."

Abraham Lincoln was among those resisting the idea of black soldiers at first. He had no love for slavery, but neither was he a believer in racial equality.

"In arguably his worst racial moment," said David Blight, author of "Race and Reunion: The Civil War in American Memory," Lincoln addressed black ministers in 1862:

"I will say then that I am not, nor ever have been, in favor of bringing about in any way the social and political equality of the white and black races; I am not nor ever have been in favor of making voters or jurors of negroes, nor of qualifying them to hold office, nor to intermarry with white people...."

He, like many other white leaders, believed that foreign colonies populated by black emigrants would solve the postwar race question.

Frederick Douglass, a former slave and guiding intellectual, was having none of it.

"Once let the black man get upon his person the brass letter, U.S., let him get an eagle on his button, and a musket on his shoulder and bullets in his pocket," he said, "there is no power on earth that can deny that he has earned the right to citizenship." In manpower-short Kansas, Sen. James Lane already had begun recruiting former slaves for an all-black unit, with even a few black officers, another breakthrough. Lt. Patrick Henry Minor's role at Island Mound appears to make him the nation's first black officer to lead members of his race in battle. The black soldiers are said to have sung...

*Once a slave but now we're free,*
*marchin' in the infantry.*
*So lift your heads and hold dem high,*
*The 1st Kansas Colored is passin' by...*

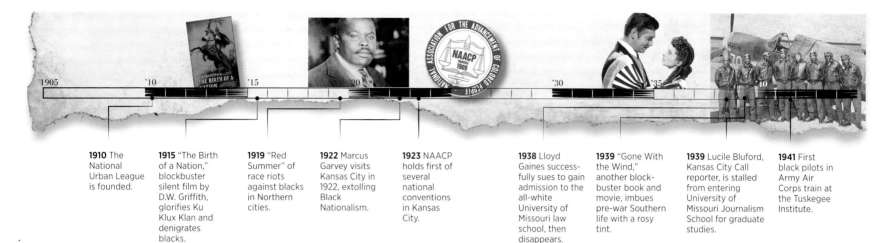

**1910** The National Urban League is founded.

**1915** "The Birth of a Nation," blockbuster silent film by D.W. Griffith, glorifies Ku Klux Klan and denigrates blacks.

**1919** "Red Summer" of race riots against blacks in Northern cities.

**1922** Marcus Garvey visits Kansas City in 1922, extolling Black Nationalism.

**1923** NAACP holds first of several national conventions in Kansas City.

**1938** Lloyd Gaines successfully sues to gain admission to the all-white University of Missouri law school, then disappears.

**1939** "Gone With the Wind," another blockbuster book and movie, imbues pre-war Southern life with a rosy tint.

**1939** Lucile Bluford, Kansas City Call reporter, is stalled from entering University of Missouri Journalism School for graduate studies.

**1941** First black pilots in Army Air Corps train at the Tuskegee Institute.

---

That fall in 1862 they occupied the Toothman farm, put up some rough breastworks, dubbed it Fort Africa. Rebel irregulars rode up; the raw recruits came out and fought them off.

The Kansas unit, not even officially mustered in, lost eight men that day — six black, one Cherokee and one white officer. All but the white officer are buried here, but no stone marks the spot. That could change with plans to declare Island Mound a historic site.

By the time the 1st Kansas Colored was breathing powder smoke outside Butler, the thinking of Lincoln and others in the North had evolved.

The Union Army had been bled in a series of defeats, but Lincoln needed more than just new regiments. He wanted to take a higher moral ground to discourage European support of Richmond and slavery.

He revealed his intention to a divided Cabinet in mid-1862, but had to wait months for a Union victory so his plan wouldn't be seen as desperation.

The Battle of Antietam offered his chance, and on Jan. 1, 1863, Lincoln issued the Emancipation Order, in some ways one of the strangest seminal documents of our history.

It would free 3.1 million of the nation's 4 million slaves, but only those held in the deep South, most of whom were beyond federal reach.

Those in bondage in Missouri, Kentucky and Maryland, all under federal control, had to wait two more years. Lincoln needed every border state Unionist — including many holding slaves. He did urge the states toward their own gradual emancipations.

"Northern generals came to realize the huge advantage they had if they recruited black soldiers," said Jimmy Johnson, a Kansas City archaeologist and high school history teacher. Unrelated to Willadina Johnson, he said his great-grandfather George Washington, a Platte County slave who escaped to Quindaro, Kan.,

also joined the 1st Kansas Colored.

For Johnson, who dresses as a Union soldier to make presentations based on the life of his ancestor, the Civil War should be celebrated for "the transition from that African-American slave to that African-American soldier."

Before the war ended, 163 black units were formed; one out of every eight Union soldiers was black. And Lincoln heard himself called "Father Abraham" by the freed slaves.

"When the war comes up, many turn off because they think all blacks did was sit around as slaves and wait for whites to save them," Joelouis Mattox, a volunteer at the Bruce R. Watkins Cultural Heritage Center, said of young African-Americans in Kansas City. "Some people do not know that 200,000 black men and women fought for their freedom — they fought like devils from hell to free their brothers and sisters."

Even when wearing Union blue, however, black

**1947** Jackie Robinson breaks baseball color barrier.

**1948** President Truman orders U.S. military to desegregate.

**1954** In Brown v. Topeka Board of Education, high court throws out "separate but equal." 19 U.S. senators and 81 congressmen urge Southern resistance.

**1955** Rosa Parks refuses to move from her bus seat and sets off the Montgomery Bus Boycott.

**1957** The Rev. Martin Luther King Jr. helps found the Southern Christian Leadership Conference.

**1957** U.S. Army paratroopers protect "Little Rock Nine," the first black students in Central High School.

**1962** Nation of Islam's Malcolm X rejects nonviolent civil-rights movement.

**1963** March on Washington; King delivers "I Have a Dream" speech.

**1963** Four girls killed in bombing of black church in Birmingham, Ala.

**1964** Civil Rights Act is passed.

**1965** Televised police violence against march in Selma, Ala., shocks nation.

**1967** Thurgood Marshall, an NAACP lawyer, is named first African-American Supreme Court justice.

**1968** King is assassinated in Memphis.

soldiers were treated differently. At first they were given lower pay than their white counterparts and had to pay for their uniforms, which whites did not.

Nor, said Jimmy Johnson, "were they used as efficiently as they could have been."

This new force often was relegated to wagon driving, grave digging, cooking and garrison duty in captured Southern towns. But while many units were assigned to such labor, thousands reached the battlefields. More than 20 black soldiers and sailors received the Medal of Honor.

"They were the bridge builders to our service today," said Maj. Clinton L. Lee, Jr., operations officer for the 15th Military Police Brigade. "I get goose bumps when I talk about it. If they hadn't gone through what they went through there is no way in the world someone like myself would be in the position that I am in today."

The award-winning 1989 film "Glory," based on the heroic attack on Fort Wagner in South Carolina by the 54th Massachusetts Colored Infantry, brought present-day attention to the black soldier's significance in the Civil War.

Besides often getting substandard supplies and inadequate medical treatment, the black soldier faced one terrible hardship that his white comrades did not — the chance of slaughter by Confederate soldiers if captured.

At Poison Springs in Arkansas, 117 men of the 1st Kansas, renamed the U.S. 79th Colored, were killed, many after being wounded or captured.

The 79th got its revenge at the Battle of Jenkins Ferry, Ark., crying, "Remember Poison Springs!" as it charged.

"The war did give African-Americans a sense of pride and dignity and that they were a part of saving the Union," said Antonio F. Holland, co-author of "Missouri's Black Heritage."

Johnson agreed that without the service of black troops in the Civil War, "then black soldiers in future wars would not have had the precedence."

African-Americans would serve in every conflict since, although in segregated units for many decades. After each overseas duty, however, they returned home with an ever stronger sense that it was their country as well that they had fought for, pushing black pride and civil rights ahead in each generation.

Yet, the argument that African-Americans made poor soldiers would be heard as late as the Korean War, most commonly from the many Southerners in the officer corps. It was President Harry Truman, who grew up not far from Butler, who ended segregation in the U.S. military.

"We remember very well how our people were treated, and we know that was just a stigma placed on them," Lee said. "But it does not stop me from knowing that I can achieve any level in today's Army.

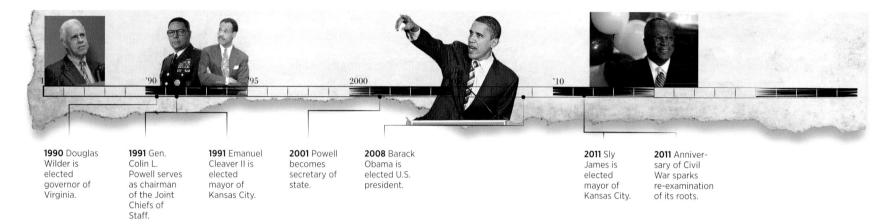

**1990** Douglas Wilder is elected governor of Virginia.

**1991** Gen. Colin L. Powell serves as chairman of the Joint Chiefs of Staff.

**1991** Emanuel Cleaver II is elected mayor of Kansas City.

**2001** Powell becomes secretary of state.

**2008** Barack Obama is elected U.S. president.

**2011** Sly James is elected mayor of Kansas City.

**2011** Anniversary of Civil War sparks re-examination of its roots.

We've had blacks on just about every level in the military today."

Of the 1.4 million people now serving on active duty in the Armed Forces, 209,356, or about 18 percent, are listed as African-American.

Gen. Colin Powell served as the first black chairman of the Joint Chiefs of Staff during the First Gulf War.

And today the commander-in-chief is President Barack Obama, widely praised for ordering a bold military operation that rid the world of Osama bin Laden.

★ ★ ★

Up a slight hill from Old Atherton Road, tiny orange flags stick up from the soil, property once owned by Jabez Smith, at one point Missouri's largest slave owner.

The flags indicate the burials of what are believed to have been more than 200 slaves, many the victims of cholera.

Jackson County's slave population grew from 193 in 1830 to 3,944 by 1860, but it was not the highest in the state. Lafayette County next door held 6,374.

The institution began here in 1720 when the first 500 slaves were dragged from Santo Domingo to toil in the lead mines around St. Louis.

By 1860, it was 115,000 slaves, about one-tenth the population, the lowest ratio of any slave state but Delaware. Then, the state auditor set their value at $44 million. Prime male slaves sold for $1,300; females fetched maybe $1,000.

The Missouri auctioneers' cry was heard most often in St. Louis, but slaves were sold, too, on the old courthouse steps in Independence and at what is now Pioneer Park at Westport Road and Broadway.

"Slavery was a business, pure and simple," said Holland.

In 1861, Mississippi's Lucius Lamar made that clear: "A blow at slavery is a blow at commerce and civilization .... We must either submit to degradation, and to the loss of property worth four billions of money, or we must secede from the Union."

At a meeting of the Civil War Roundtable of Western Missouri, a member blurted, "Here in Missouri we treated our slaves good, in many cases like family."

Diane Mutti Burke, a University of Missouri-Kansas City history professor and that evening's lecturer, was polite, but later chuckled.

"There's nothing ever good about owning another human being, about slavery," she said.

Take Henry Clay Bruce, a slave who was never whipped by his owner, according to his memoir. But on neighboring farms, he noted, "someone was whipped nearly every week."

Four out of five African-Americans today descended from enslaved ancestors.

The great-great-grandfather of Willadine Johnson, Company E. Cpl. Rufus Vann, fought with the 1st Kansas Colored Volunteer Infantry and is buried at the Little Rock (Ark.) National Cemetery. At left, a statue in honor of those soldiers stands on the courthouse square in Butler, Mo.

PHOTOS BY KEITH MYERS, THE KANSAS CITY STAR

"There is a lot of pain to think about the inhumanities and the indignities of slavery," explained Marc Morial, president of the National Urban League. "There is a human instinct, which says I want to forget that pain; I want to move beyond that pain."

The Federal victory saw freedom inked onto paper in the words of the 13th, 14th and 15th amendments.

But it did not prevent a whole new bucket of mean heaved at black Americans. Without money, property or education, their new freedoms often proved empty, indeed.

"There was great optimism on the part of the freed people that after the Civil War, they would get their 40 acres and a mule, and the yearning of democracy would be opened to them," said Mary Frances Berry, history professor at the University of Pennsylvania and former chairwoman of the U.S. Commission on Civil Rights.

"But that land dream did not come to fruition," she said.

To many, the oppressive sharecropping economy would seem little better than slave days. The Ku Klux Klan, led by former Confederate Lt. Gen. Nathan Bedford Forrest, initiated a wave of terror.

"The values that the South fought for, their way of life, which is the exploitation of African-Americans and the denigation of African-Americans, became the values of the North," said Ajamu K. Webster, chairman of the Kansas City Black United Front.

"The North won the war but the South won the peace."

★ ★ ★

The backlash against the black community, Morial calls "One of the great tragedies throughout history ... a deep, deep betrayal to the important victories that the Civil War was meant to produce."

In 1877, as part of a political deal that ended a presidential election dispute, Reconstruction policies and federal occupation were lifted from the Southern states. Many "redeemer" laws were quickly passed to restore white supremacy and black disenfranchisement.

"In Plessy v. Ferguson, the values that the South fought and stood for became the law of the land. It took another 100 years for us to get to where we are today," Webster said.

The court case upheld what became the "Jim Crow" racial caste system that lasted into the 1960s. Across the South, "White only" signs hung everywhere. Sharing cafes, shops, hotels, trains, classes, water fountains and prison cells was prohibited. Black accommodations almost always were below the standards reserved for white Americans.

A person of color could not ride in the front seat of a car driven by a white; if it was a truck, the black person rode in the back. At intersections, the black driver did not have the right-of-way.

A black man could not offer to shake the hand of a white man, could not accuse him of lying, could not laugh at him. Blacks could not kiss in public; it offended whites. Kissing a white women meant death.

Joelouis Mattox grew up in Missouri's boot heel, the cotton country around Caruthersville, "a community where black people survived because we knew our place and we stayed in our place."

"We had colored schools and got accustomed to the secondhand books," Mattox said. "Blacks could not swim in the public swimming pool, and we swam in the Mississippi River. We were told by our teachers that we had to be better than our white counterparts because of the color of our skin. Our teachers instilled in us we could be somebody, and we did not have to stay there and take it.

"However, it was not the worst place to live. Sikeston and New Madrid were much worse. Sikeston had (Missouri's) last reported lynching of a black person in 1942."

Between 1889 and 1918, more than 2,500 black men were hanged, shot or burned by mobs. In 1901, a bill to make lynching a federal crime was proposed. Southerners in Congress blocked it for more than 50 years.

Race riots sparked by whites broke out from New Orleans to Chicago. If law officers did not join in, then they stood by. In the early 1920s, thriving black communities in Tulsa's Greenwood district and Rosewood, Fla., were wiped out.

"We are still dealing with the aftermath of the Civil War as a nation," said Darryck Dean, president of Harmony, a Kansas City non-profit agency that promotes diversity and improved race relations. "If you look at the legacy of the war, Reconstruction, Jim Crow and so forth, we are still trying to correct the wrongs the South sought to keep."

Roughly a century after the war, many enlisted in

a second civil conflict, again, largely in the South.

Its battles included voter registration, sit-ins, bus boycotts, paratroopers escorting students, church bombings, police dogs and fire hoses, equal rights and voting rights laws, an "I Have a Dream" speech under Lincoln's gaze and much, much more.

"Young African-Americans and the public in general must know that when we look at the Civil War and civil rights movement, there were many white people who stood on the side of freedom and died to make men free," said Mattox.

Yet, with the gains, segregation is still found across the nation. Black Americans suffer economic difficulties disproportionately, still find their children in substandard schools.

"With all the sacrifices that have been made over the last 150 years, look where we are today," said Gilmore. "We have a black man in the Oval Office, being called out in the middle of him giving a national speech; and being challenged about whether he was actually born in this country."

Nothing points to the centrality of race to our past as much as the Civil War, said activist Julian Bond, grandson of a Kentucky slave.

"And nothing forces us to acknowledge its continued centrality to our present more than the refusal by some, after 150 years, to admit that the war was about slavery.

"Those who say that 'race is history' have it exactly backward," he said. "History is race. The word America' scrambled, after all, spells 'I am race.'"

**After denying African-Americans a chance to fight against slavery in the first months of the war, the Lincoln administration came around and by early 1863 was recruiting them by the thousands. Before the war was over, more than 200,000 wore the blue uniform, and of those, at least 40,000 made the ultimate sacrifice.**

| ILLUSTRATION FROM "THE SOLDIER IN OUR CIVIL WAR," 1885, COURTESY OF THE MISSOURI VALLEY ROOM, KANSAS CITY LIBRARY

# SLAVERY, 'THE ORIGINAL SIN OF THE FOUNDERS,' HAS LONG CONFOUND

By MARÁ ROSE WILLLIAMS ★ THE KANSAS CITY STAR

After 150 years, the place of slavery, that "peculiar institution," in our history still makes many of us uncomfortable.

When Virginia Gov. Robert F. McDonnell's Confederate History Month proclamation attracted unhappy attention last year by omitting slavery from issues "significant" to the state, he amended it.

Also in Virginia, a teacher held a mock slave auction in which the white 10-year-olds bought their black and mixed-race classmates.

Parents were not amused.

Rep. Michele Bachmann of Minnesota, a possible GOP presidential candidate, made another history gaffe saying: "the very founders that wrote those documents worked tirelessly until slavery was no more in the United States."

As many pointed out, Thomas Jefferson, George Washington and Patrick Henry — who said, "Give me liberty or give me death" — all slave owners, did nothing of the sort.

"What is critically important is to understand that the nation fought a very costly war to create a more perfect union," said David Blight, a Yale University history professor, "to end the original sin of the founders ... a stain on the Constitution."

While the Declaration of Independence proclaimed that all men are created equal, it did not apply to the thousands enslaved along the Eastern Seaboard.

A lost Manhattan Island cemetery found in 2003 reminded us that 18th century New York had more slaves than any city but Charleston, S.C.

Even after the North shed the practice, its industries — from textile mills to shipping to banking and insurance — still sipped profits from the sweat of slaves.

The institution actually had begun to decline in the South as well — until "King Cotton" began its rule and demanded more and more land and the labor to work it.

"Contrary to conventional wisdom, and the lessons taught in schools, the War Between the States was not fought to end slavery," said Walter E. Williams, a professor at George Mason University who is African-American. Instead, he contended, it was tariffs and Northern aggression trampling states' rights.

"Yeah, it was..." responded Blight. "States' rights to own slaves."

The crisis was provoked by the election of Abraham Lincoln, who insisted to a disbelieving South that he had neither legal authority nor intention to dismantle slavery.

But Lincoln would not brook any more expansion westward.

"That, I suppose, is the rub," he wrote.

The rub was rawest in "Bleeding Kansas." Historians refer to this period as the Civil War's first act.

In a recent Time magazine essay, David Von Drehle agreed, quoting John Brown, notorious in 1850s Kansas for massacring five pro-slavery men at Pottawatomie Creek.

"In Kansas, the question is never raised of a man: Is he a Democrat? Is he a Republican? The questions there raised are: Is he a Free State man? Or is he a pro-slavery man?"

As Von Drehle noted: "This is why armies marched."

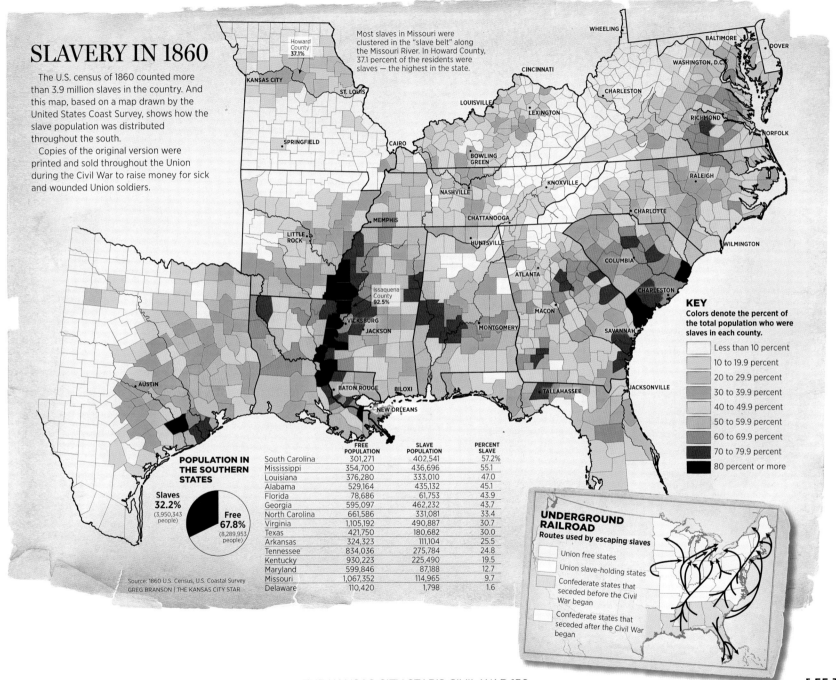

# SLAVERY IN 1860

The U.S. census of 1860 counted more than 3.9 million slaves in the country. And this map, based on a map drawn by the United States Coast Survey, shows how the slave population was distributed throughout the south.

Copies of the original version were printed and sold throughout the Union during the Civil War to raise money for sick and wounded Union soldiers.

Most slaves in Missouri were clustered in the "slave belt" along the Missouri River. In Howard County, 37.1 percent of the residents were slaves — the highest in the state.

Howard County 37.1%

Issaquena County 92.5%

## KEY

Colors denote the percent of the total population who were slaves in each county.

- Less than 10 percent
- 10 to 19.9 percent
- 20 to 29.9 percent
- 30 to 39.9 percent
- 40 to 49.9 percent
- 50 to 59.9 percent
- 60 to 69.9 percent
- 70 to 79.9 percent
- 80 percent or more

## POPULATION IN THE SOUTHERN STATES

Slaves **32.2%** (3,950,343 people)

Free **67.8%** (8,289,953 people)

| | FREE POPULATION | SLAVE POPULATION | PERCENT SLAVE |
|---|---|---|---|
| South Carolina | 301,271 | 402,541 | 57.2% |
| Mississippi | 354,700 | 436,696 | 55.1 |
| Louisiana | 376,280 | 333,010 | 47.0 |
| Alabama | 529,164 | 435,132 | 45.1 |
| Florida | 78,686 | 61,753 | 43.9 |
| Georgia | 595,097 | 462,232 | 43.7 |
| North Carolina | 661,586 | 331,081 | 33.4 |
| Virginia | 1,105,192 | 490,887 | 30.7 |
| Texas | 421,750 | 180,682 | 30.0 |
| Arkansas | 324,323 | 111,104 | 25.5 |
| Tennessee | 834,036 | 275,784 | 24.8 |
| Kentucky | 930,223 | 225,490 | 19.5 |
| Maryland | 599,846 | 87,188 | 12.7 |
| Missouri | 1,067,352 | 114,965 | 9.7 |
| Delaware | 110,420 | 1,798 | 1.6 |

Source: 1860 U.S. Census, U.S. Coastal Survey
GREG BRANSON | THE KANSAS CITY STAR

## UNDERGROUND RAILROAD

Routes used by escaping slaves

- Union free states
- Union slave-holding states
- Confederate states that seceded before the Civil War began
- Confederate states that seceded after the Civil War began

# Descendants of slave and owner bond

By MARÁ ROSE WILLLIAMS ★ THE KANSAS CITY STAR

**GENERATIONS**
**A series of family memories about local ancestors in the Civil War.**

Until Corrine Patterson was in her 70s, her great-grandfather Jeremiah McCanse was pretty much a stranger to her. And Janet McCanse Mundy was completely unknown to her.

Now the long-dead former slave and Civil War soldier shares her dining room table.

And the white woman in Belton is a part of her life.

Recently, Patterson moved to the corner of the table where the white, plastic binders stuffed with laminated pieces of history are stacked. She flipped through them to find McCanse's military pension papers.

And there, in the flowing script of an unknown bureaucrat, are exposed the bare bones of Jeremiah's war.

Freed in 1863 by his owner in Mount Vernon, Mo.

Enlisted at age 16 in Springfield, Mo., in the 113th U.S. Colored Infantry, a regiment organized in Arkansas.

Played drum and fife in Company A. Wounded in the leg, possibly by a bayonet, and sent to the hospital. He recovered from the injury and resultant

Corinne Patterson (from left), Janey McCanse Munday and Alberta McCanse Goode talked recently about the warm relationship they have developed. | KEITH MYERS, THE KANSAS CITY STAR

fever but was bothered by residual pain throughout his adult life.

Mustered out in Arkansas in 1866.

"I wish my parents and grandmother had told me about him," said Patterson, 84. "I don't know why they didn't tell me. It never dawned on me to ask."

But her cousin, Alberta McCanse Goode, had heard all about Grandpa Jeremiah, a fairly well-known barber in Spring Hill, Kan., where he died in 1904.

He owned two buildings in the town, both of which still stand, and was the first black man to sit on the school board. A savvy businessman, he lured customers from other shops by playing a phonograph while cutting hair.

"My daddy told me about my grandpa," said Goode, of Kansas City. "But I was a kid, and I didn't think anything more about it."

Not until the day she spotted a Kansas City Star article about local African-Americans being considered for a mural depicting Spring Hill history. The article appeared with a photo of Jeremiah McCanse. Goode called Patterson.

Goode, 79, wasn't the only one to recognize the gray-haired man.

"We knew who he was," said Mundy.

She and twin Andy McCanse are great-grandchildren to William McCanse, merchant, farmer and Lawrence County treasurer in the 1880s. His farm was worked by nine slaves.

"My great-granddaddy — they called him Uncle Billy — had some papers, and it listed all his property and how much they were worth," Mundy said.

**Jeremiah McCanse**

**William McCanse**

The name of Jeremiah, who, like many slaves, took the owner's name, was there with the others. A child, he was valued at $600.

"We knew he'd gone on to be successful," said the 82-year-old Belton woman. "He once sent the family a letter. My granddaddy taught them all to read, I suspect. His letter said he was doing well. I remember he said he had the gayest garden in Kansas."

Contacts with the newspaper soon connected descendants of the slave with descendants of the slave owner. The families, separated by race and time, had lived only 20 minutes away from one another their entire lives.

Today they talk often by telephone and get together at family affairs as if their connection were blood.

"Who knows? Maybe it is," said Mundy.

Then she leaned to wrap her arms around Goode. The two giggled like schoolgirls and hugged.

From the moment the families met at her home in 2001, said Patterson, "it never seemed strange to me at all."

Together they even erected a new headstone on Jeremiah's grave. The old stone had misspelled his name.

"I don't put all slave owners in the same boat," Patterson said. "I believe the way they treat me now is the way they treated them back during that time, like family. Obviously they weren't all cruel."

"What's color got to do with anything anyway?" Goode asked. "We have a great time together. We don't see color. And anyone with a heart would feel the same way we do."

# HOW DEEP THE RANKS OF 'FORGOTTEN' BLACK REBELS?

By MARÁ ROSE WILLLIAMS ★ THE KANSAS CITY STAR

That black men, slaves and freedmen alike, served their homeland — the Confederate States of America — is beyond dispute. But how many? And in what capacity?

With the 150th anniversary of the Civil War, the "Forgotten Confederate," or the myth of him, has risen again.

Some contend that 60,000 served the rebel cause. Mostly behind the lines in support roles, of course, but a few got up front where the bullets flew.

"Whatever the job, if you did it for the Army, you were a soldier," said Walter Williams, African-American economics professor at George Mason University. He argues for the inclusion of the 60,000 blacks among the 750,000 to 900,000 Confederate troops.

To which Hari Jones scoffed.

"You will never find documentation for that number because that 60,000 never existed," said the curator of the National African-American Civil War Memorial and Museum in Washington, D.C. He believes, "at most," about 1,500 black men did

service, although not gun-toting, in the CSA ranks.

Jones said his museum has found Confederate records for about a dozen who were mustered in as cooks or musicians in North Carolina regiments.

"In the field, officers needed soldiers, and they didn't care whether they had enlistment papers," replied retired Lt. Col. Edwin L. Kennedy Jr., who teaches history at the Command and General Staff College at Fort Leavenworth. To him, 60,000 is a fair estimate.

"If they are shooting a musket, then who cares if they are on the enlistment rolls?"

On both sides, trenches had to be dug, fortifications raised, supply wagons driven, mules shod, meals cooked, laundry done and music played. But the South, outnumbered on the front 2-to-1 and always short of manpower, used thousands of slaves were contracted to the government. And Southern officers had black servants in the field.

"Black men have volunteered to serve their country in all our wars," said Williams. "To ignore the black Confederate soldier is to do dishonor to him."

Jones: "Let's not call them anything other than what they were — Confederate slaves. The Confederates used slave labor."

In the 25,000 soldiers' letters he read for his Pulitzer Prizewinning "Battle Cry of Freedom: The Civil War Era," James McPherson found mention of only about a dozen black soldiers among the rebels.

For the existence of 60,000 — the equivalent of roughly five divisions — Jones finds few "enlistment papers, nothing to prove they ever existed."

To advocates of the "Forgotten Confederates," who argue that Northern victors got to rewrite history their way, that is not surprising. A few will go as far as to claim such records and photographs were purged by those who did not wish to acknowledge the black men.

The notion of thousands of black Confederates buttresses the contention that the war was over state sovereignty, not slavery. If the Southern way of life was so bad, why did so many of these men of color join the rebellion alongside white comrades?

During the late 1850s, Williams explained, "peo-

**Once the war began, escaping slaves looking for freedom began showing up in Federal camps. At first, Union officers were not sure what to do with them and even returned some to their owners, Soon, however, the African-Americans were seen as "contraband," that is property to be taken from the southerners to hamper their war effort. The name stuck and the black fugitives became known as contrabands. In Missouri, thousands fled to Kansas.** | ILLUSTRATION FROM "THE SOLDIER IN OUR CIVIL WAR," 1885, COURTESY OF THE MISSOURI VALLEY ROOM, KANSAS CITY LIBRARY

ple didn't consider themselves as citizens of the U.S. They saw their state as their country. These blacks who were slaves, some of them freedmen, saw their country under attack and were willing to defend it. ... Because of their loyalty, they would be treated better after the war."

Entrusting hundreds or thousands of black men to take up arms, however, ran counter to the South's deep-rooted fear of slave uprisings.

Evidence of black men actually fighting in rebel ranks is largely anecdotal. One Union officer held prisoner complained bitterly that he had thought he was fighting to free the Negro who held a shotgun at his head. In 1862, a Union doctor reported seeing "over 3,000 negroes ... clad in all manner of uniforms" during a rebel occupation of Frederick, Md., but he tended to greatly exaggerate troop numbers.

"Better Confederates did not live," said Gen. Nathan Bedford Forrest.

Before the war a slave trader, after it the first Grand Wizard of the Ku Klux Klan, Forrest took 45 slaves into the cavalry with him, promising them freedom, either way it turned out.

In Missouri, three black men, apparently all freedmen, served at times with guerrilla chief William Quantrill. John Noland even attended postwar Bushwhacker reunions and was carried to his grave by six white pallbearers.

In 1897, The Kansas City Star wrote of Billy Hunter, once owned by Missouri's famous Confederate cavalry commander, Gen. Jo Shelby.

"Billy rode forth at the side of his gallant, young master," who, the story said, outfitted Hunter in a gray uniform.

> *Evidence of black men actually fighting in rebel ranks is largely anecdotal. One Union officer held prisoner complained bitterly that he had thought he was fighting to free the Negro who held a shotgun at his head.*

The slave carried the general's weapons, besides cooking for him. But, as Hunter told his interviewer, he was "what you call a high private in the rear ranks most times. Been knocked with a skillet or a piece of fence rail and run over by horses and shot at, but I never shot."

Perhaps hundreds of such body servants accompanied their masters to war. James G. Hollandsworth Jr., a former professor at the University of Southern Mississippi, researched state pension archives and found that 85 percent of black applicants were servants or cooks. They served in every theater of the war, and he assumes some did so willingly.

Only at the very end did the Confederacy consider enlisting and arming its slaves. Gen. Robert E. Lee favored the idea. Virginia adopted it.

The Richmond Enquirer opined: "The question of making soldiers of Negroes, of regularly enlisting them, for their own safety as well as our own, must have presented itself to every reflecting mind. Because the Yankees have not been able to make soldiers out of their drafted Negroes, it does not follow that we cannot train our slaves to make very efficient troops. We believe that they can be, by drill and discipline, molded into steady and reliable soldiers."

The experiment was tried, but the war ended weeks later.

Steven Woodworth, a professor at Texas Christian University, knew of one New Orleans black militia unit that volunteered service to the rebels. They were rejected.

When the Yankees occupied the city midway in the war, the militia went to their side.

# Quindaro served slaves as station on freedom's route

By **GLENN E. RICE** ★ THE KANSAS CITY STAR

Viewing the few ruins of old Quindaro, it is difficult to imagine the bustling river town of the 1850s where steamboats tied up. Pieces of mortared limestone nearly lost in the brush were the Quindaro House, a five-story hotel. On the path's other side, impressive footings show where a warehouse once stood.

At the better-preserved brewery is an arched cellar for cooling the product.

And for hiding the runaway slaves, it is said.

For Quindaro was a station on the Underground Railroad.

At night, slaves slipped away to this haven, braving whippings from patrols on the east side of the Missouri River and fearing the catchers who stalked them on the west side for a master's bounty.

"People who were born, bred and raised right here have no clue of the enormity, gravity or the depth of the sacrifice that was made here by those towards their pursuit to freedom," said Marvin Robinson, one of many who work to preserve the Quindaro site.

The Underground Railroad operated as an infor-

Jimmy Johnson, a local high school teacher, recently gave a tour of what
was Quindaro, Kan., a station on the Underground Railroad. | TODD FEEBACK, THE KANSAS CITY STAR

mal, secret network to help escaped slaves reach Northern states or Canada.

At its "stations," sympathetic souls and brave hearts, the "conductors," would hide them, feed them and help them on their way.

Quindaro briefly flourished as a secure river port for the passengers and cargo of the New England Emigrant Aid Co.

Wyandott City, Leavenworth and Atchison at that time were filled with pro-slavery men from Missouri.

As a result, Quindaro was closely linked to Lawrence, the epicenter of the Free Staters. There, in early 1858, Samuel Tappan wrote to a Massachusetts minister: "I am happy to inform you that a certain Rail Road has been and is in full blast. Several persons have taken full advantage of it."

At least two got there in large wooden boxes in a jolting wagon, according to resident Clarina I.H. Nichols, who wrote in 1882 how "Uncle Tom's boys could tell of some exciting escapes from Quindaro to the interior, by day and by night."

Nichols recalled taking home to Vermont a pair of manacles filed from a runaway from around Parkville, "having drawn one foot from the encircling iron and brought the chain still attached to the other, in his hand. The man having learned that he was sold south attempted to escape and was at once put in irons."

While she boasted that only one man was recaptured by the slave hunters who camped nearby, in what is now Quindaro Park, records show a young woman also was dragged back to Missouri.

In late October 1861, Nichols said, a fugitive named Caroline hid in her dry cistern, lowered there with

A Quindaro statue honors John Brown.

rocking chair, blankets and pillows.

"But poor Caroline trembling and almost paralyzed with fear of discovery her nerves weakened by grieving for her little girl transported to Texas, and the cruel blows which had broken her arm and scarred her body could not be left. ...

"All night I crept to and fro in slippered feet ... whispering words of cheer to Caroline in her cell, and back again to watch and wait and whisper."

The slavers finally rode out at 7 a.m.

"When evening fell again, Caroline and another

girl of whom the hunters were in pursuit found safe conveyance to Leavenworth friends."

That might have been William Mathews, a black owner of a hostel there.

"All stations were important and critical if you were an escaping person," said Tim Wescott, a history professor at Park University.

Having researched escape routes here, he said no one knows how many runaways passed through Quindaro.

The legends say the slaves would reach a spot called "Happy Hollow" and drop to their knees to rejoice and pray. Another story is of "Bell Landing," where the ringing let folks know fugitives had arrived.

Many came in small boats, letting the current ground them on the river's curve.

The river then was much wider and shallower, with shifting sandbars and islands. The current was much slower. A night swim might be risked at low water. In winter, the slaves simply waited until the freeze and then walked over the ice.

Although Missouri's Black Codes severely fined a ferryman for carrying a slave, Quindaro's steam ferry apparently made secret runs — until angry Missourians sank it in 1861.

The town reached a population of around 1,200, but it went into a steep decline and was only about half that by 1860. Poorly situated in rough hills, it was largely unneeded once the pro-slavery crowd and their "Bogus Laws" were rejected from Kansas.

Its ruins are just west of Interstate 635 before it crosses the river. At the end of 37th Street, a recently built gazebo overlooks some of the site.

## A SOLDIER WRITES TO HIS GIRLS:

# 'GOD NEVER INTENDED FOR MAN TO STEAL HIS OWN BLOOD'

*On Sept. 3, 1864, a soldier at Benton Barracks Hospital in St. Louis sent a reassuring letter to his children upriver in Glasgow, a scene repeated thousands of times over the long course of the war. But in this case, the soldier, Pvt. Spotswood Rice, told his daughters to be patient, that he would come to free them. The same day, Rice — once a subservient slave, now a confident Union infantryman — sent another letter — to Kitty Diggs, the woman who owned his children, "that the longor you keep my Child from me the longor you will have to burn in hell and the qwicer you get their."*

My Children I take my pen in hand to rite you A few lines to let you know that I have not forgot you and that I want to see you as bad as ever now my Dear Children I want you to be contented with whatever may be your lots be assured that I will have you if it cost me my life on the 28th of the mounth. 8 hundred White and 8 hundred blacke solders expet to start up the revore to Glasgow and above the thats to be jeneraled by a jeneral that will give me both of you when they Come I expect to be with them and expect to get you both in return.

Dont be uneasy my children I expect to have you. If Diggs dont give you up this Government will and I feel confident that I will get you Your

Miss Kaitty said that I tried to steal you. But I'll let her know that god never intended for man to steal his own flesh and blood. If I had no confidence in God I could have confidence in her. But as it is If I ever had any Con- fidence in her I have none now and never ex- pect to have. And I want her to remember if she meets me with ten thousands soldiers she (will) meet her enemy I once (thought) that I had some respect for them but now my respects is worn

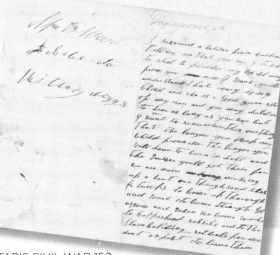

out and have no sympathy for Slaveholders. And as for her cristianantty I expect the Devil has Such in hell You tell her from me that She is the frist Christian that I ever had say that a man could Steal his own child especially out of human bondage.

You can tell her that She can hold to you as long as she can. I never would expect to ask her again to let you come to me because I know that the devil has got her hot set againsts that that is write. now my Dear children I am going to close my letter to you. Give my love to all enquiring friends tell them all that we are well and want to see them very much and Corra and Mary receive the greater part of it you sefves and dont think hard of us not sending you any thing. I you father have a plenty for you when I see you ... Oh! My Dear children how I do want to see you ...

# Family farms didn't represent a better system of slavery

Missouri slavery differed significantly from the images of large cotton and rice plantations, complete with the big house and slave quarters, which have come to represent the Old South.

The profile of most Missouri slaveholdings reflected the family farm rather than the plantation: Nearly 90 percent of slaveholders owned 10 or fewer slaves. Farming families generally worked alongside their few slaves as they practiced the diversified agriculture common to the region.

Not long after the Civil War, white Missourians began to recall that their ancestors treated black people like "members of the family." They described Missouri slavery as humane — in spite of the more critical picture painted by those who had actually endured enslavement.

**AUTHOR'S ESSAY**

**Diane Mutti Burke** wrote "On Slavery's Borders: Small Slaveholding in Antebellum Missouri." A professor of history at the University of Missouri-Kansas City, she is a graduate of Emory University, Dartmouth College and Oak Park High School in Kansas City.

The interactions between slaves and owners were more personal, but this never translated into a "better" system of bondage. Rather, the historical evidence suggests that Missouri slavery was often just as cruel and exploitative as anywhere.

A few slaveholders felt an affinity with those with whom they lived and worked so closely, and this at times resulted in kinder treatment. This intimacy worked both ways, however. Slaves were well placed to understand the personalities of their owners and use this knowledge to their advantage.

At the same time, the marginal economic conditions of small-scale slavery coupled with the tenuous nature of life on the geographic border of the slave South encouraged slave resistance and undermined the authority of owners.

Yet these interactions always occurred in a context where slaves' lives were largely beyond their control. They were subject to their owners' personalities and whims — ranging from empathy and cooperation to the worst forms of physical, sexual and psychological abuse.

What is often missed, too, is that other aspects of life on Missouri's farms could be more difficult.

Most slaves had less access to family members and the larger black community, both of which would have helped to mitigate the harshest aspects of enslavement.

Family was a priority for slaves, but finding marriage partners on their home farms was challenging.

In fact, well over half of Missouri couples participated in abroad marriages — a slave woman and her children on one farm and the husband and father on a neighbor's property. Married men customarily were allowed to visit their wives and children only once or twice a week.

In addition, families were more likely to be separated when slaves were hired out to local whites, at the settlement of deceased owner's estates, or when they were sold — sometimes literally down the river.

In spite of the many restrictions placed on them, enslaved people showed an amazing ability to adapt to their difficult circumstances and resist the dehumanizing effects of their condition by developing and sustaining strong human connections across farm boundaries.

The many risks they took and the great lengths that they went to in order to maintain friendships and family bonds demonstrate the importance of these relationships.

Given the alternative of isolation, most men, women and children accepted the limitations of abroad families and relished the little time they spent with one another. In the face of high mortality and the deprivations of slavery, families were remarkably stable.

Enslaved Missourians also took advantage of opportunities to socialize with others in the greater community. Owners actually encouraged this social interaction when it promoted their economic goals.

They routinely sent men into town on farm errands, and both men and women attended barn raisings and corn huskings. They also allowed abroad men to visit their wives in order to encourage procreation and because they believed that family ties would make them less likely to rebel or flee. Owners also took their slaves to integrated churches, where white preachers directed them to obey both their spiritual and worldly masters.

Slaveholders rarely forbade their slaves' involvement

An item sold at a probate sale with the bedsteads and the horses was "John," an 18-year-old whose life was about to be upended. He might have been worth $1,000 as a hemp cutter.

| COURTESY OF MELVIN BOCKELMAN

in the greater slave community outright, but instead attempted to closely monitor their activities and associations. Slaves carried a written pass from their owner when they left their home farm or risked brutality at the hands of the local slave patrol.

Despite their best efforts, owners never achieved complete domination. Enslaved Missourians converted white-sanctioned social occasions into sites of family and friendship, as well as music, storytelling and dance. Some sought social interactions that were free from white control and attended clandestine parties and black-led religious services in the local woods.

In spite of the tremendous challenges, remarkably, many enslaved Missourians, such as Spotswood and Orry Rice, managed to foster stable and long-lasting ties with others.

The Howard County couple began their married life in 1852 but spent the first 12 years living on separate slaveholdings. Their daughter Mary Bell described her parents as helping each another endure the "hard times" of slavery, even though they only saw one another twice a week.

Bell's father often came to them bloodied from beatings he had received at the hands of the slave driver on his master's plantation, and her mother would tend to his wounds, wash his clothes and send him back again.

Spotswood Rice eventually gained freedom through enlistment in the Union Army midway through the war and immediately set about working to bring his wife and children out of bondage. While most of his family made it to safety in St. Louis, two of his daughters remained behind.

Rice assured Corra and Mary that "I will have you if it cost me my life."

Believing the full power of the federal government and the Union Army would support him in his quest, he even threatened Mary's mistress that his girls were not her property, writing: "My Children is my own and I expect to get them."

The Rice girls eventually were reunited with their parents, and the family thrived in postwar St. Louis.

Countless Missouri slaves shared similar stories. Like the Rice family, the road out of bondage was long, but they held together as they hoped for a brighter future in freedom.

# STARS & BARS

**Southern Cross**

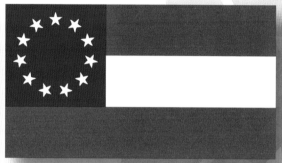

**The Stars and Bars**

**Missouri Confederate banner**

It's not, as many believe, the bumper-sticker favorite, the rebel battle flag with its star-loaded St. Andrew's cross. Originally the Virginia battle flag, that "Southern Cross" banner was adopted widely as the war progressed. The Stars and Bars had three broad stripes, two red and one white, with a circle of stars in the top-left blue-box corner, much like the U.S. flag — which was a problem on the smoky battlefield. Many Missouri Confederates actually fought under a blue banner showing a large white cross.

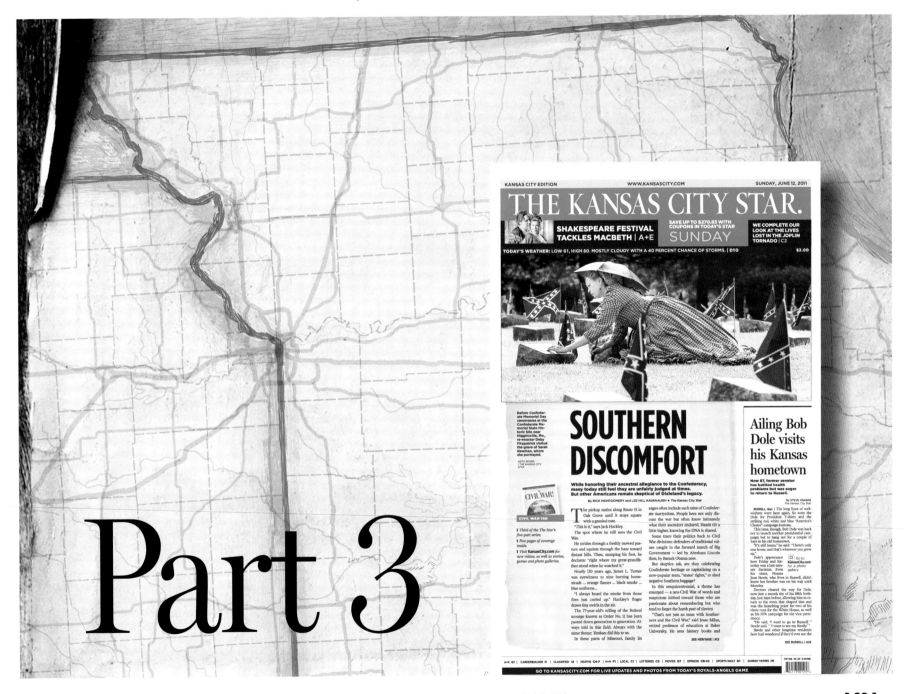

# Southern discomfort

While honoring their ancestral allegiance to the Confederacy, many today still feel they are unfairly judged at times. But other Americans remain skeptical of Dixieland's legacy.

By **RICK MONTGOMERY & LEE HILL KAVANAUGH** ★ THE KANSAS CITY STAR

The pickup rattles along Route H in Oak Grove until it stops square with a gnarled tree.

"This is it," says Jack Hackley. The spot where he still sees the Civil War. He strides through a freshly mowed pasture and squints through the haze toward distant hills. Then, stamping his foot, he declares: "right where my great-grandfather stood when he watched it."

Nearly 150 years ago, James L. Turner was eyewitness to nine burning homesteads ... orange flames ... black smoke ... blue uniforms...

"I always heard the smoke from those fires

**Before Confederate Memorial Day ceremonies at the Confederate Memorial State Historic Site near Higginsville, Mo., re-enactor Deby Fitzpatrick visited the grave of Sarah Newman, whom she portrayed.** | KEITH MYERS, THE KANSAS CITY STAR

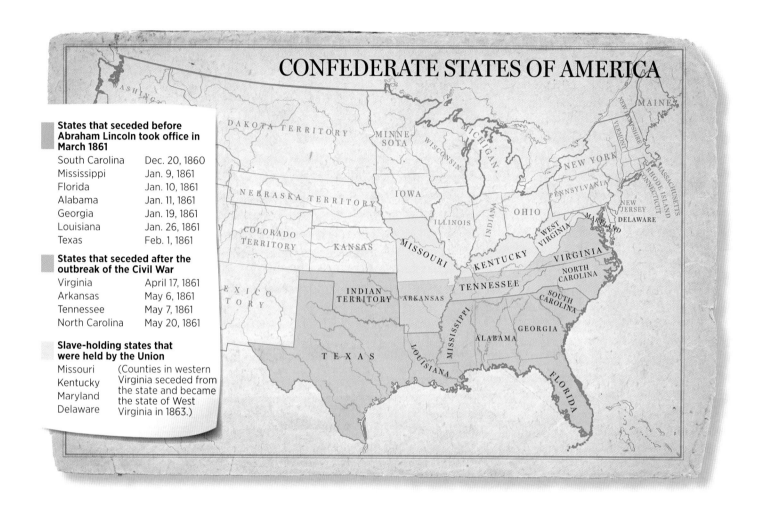

CONFEDERATE STATES OF AMERICA

**States that seceded before Abraham Lincoln took office in March 1861**

| South Carolina | Dec. 20, 1860 |
| Mississippi | Jan. 9, 1861 |
| Florida | Jan. 10, 1861 |
| Alabama | Jan. 11, 1861 |
| Georgia | Jan. 19, 1861 |
| Louisiana | Jan. 26, 1861 |
| Texas | Feb. 1, 1861 |

**States that seceded after the outbreak of the Civil War**

| Virginia | April 17, 1861 |
| Arkansas | May 6, 1861 |
| Tennessee | May 7, 1861 |
| North Carolina | May 20, 1861 |

**Slave-holding states that were held by the Union**

Missouri
Kentucky
Maryland
Delaware

(Counties in western Virginia seceded from the state and became the state of West Virginia in 1863.)

just curled up." Hackley's finger draws tiny swirls in the air.

The 77-year-old's telling of the Federal scourge known as Order No. 11 has been passed down generation to generation. Always told in this field. Always with the same theme: Yankees did this to us.

In these parts of Missouri, family lineages often include such tales of Confederate martyrdom. People here not only discuss the war but often know intimately what their ancestors endured. Heads tilt a little higher, knowing the DNA is shared.

Some trace their politics back to Civil War divisions: defenders of traditional values caught in the forward march of Big Government — led by Abraham Lincoln then, by Barack Obama now.

But skeptics ask, are they celebrating Confederate heritage or capitalizing on a now-popular term, "states' rights," to shed negative Southern baggage?

In this sesquicentennial, a theme has emerged — a neo-Civil War of words and suspicions lobbed toward those who are passionate about remembering but who tend to forget the harsh past of slavery.

"That's not just an issue with Southerners and the Civil War," said Jesse Milan, retired professor of education at Baker University. He sees history books and teachers too often ducking many issues about race. "All of U.S. history is full of denying, even in the 21st century."

Others say shame has been shackled to pride too long.

"Times have changed greatly over the last 50 years," said Bill Myrick, a Sons of Confederate Veterans camp commander speaking at an Alabama event. "Political correctness has managed to instill a false shame in so many Southerners. One has only to mutter the word 'racist' to send many into hiding."

Only 38 percent of Americans said in a Pew Research Center poll that slavery was the major cause of the fighting. The April 2011 survey showed 48 percent believe the war was mainly about states' rights. Puzzled academics digging deep into the thinking of the 1800s say, no, it was mostly about slavery.

Hackley is perplexed about it, too: "A funny thing... Out of all the stories I ever heard, no one in my family ever mentioned slavery." But he shrugs off what others may think. His ancestors, being pretty poor, probably didn't own slaves, anyway.

What the war dealt his family is sad enough.

Among the many whom great-grandfather Turner killed were his brother and a neighbor, both Union men. Years later, he tried to kill himself and spent the rest of his life in an insane asylum.

"Yeah," says Hackley, his face drawn with sadness. "You could say my family was bitter about that war.

"Still is."

## REMEMBERING

At the Midwest Genealogic Center in Independence, 14 women bow their heads for a moment of silence.

"On this day 150 years ago, at 11 a.m." says Trish Spencer, United Daughters of the Confederacy chapter president, "the war began that would eventually take more than 600,000 lives. We do this to remember them."

Next, the women pledge allegiance to a miniature U.S. flag, say an oath to the Missouri flag, and offer "undying remembrance" to the Confederate battle flag.

On their agenda is a report on their work, finding and identifying headstones of forgotten rebel veterans. Wood-lawn Cemetery in Independence, Spencer says, has 160 named Confederate graves, twice as many as previously thought.

The Daughters of the Confederacy are amateur history sleuths, piecing together entire lives from shards of information, pension records, family letters, diaries and death certificates.

Founded in 1894, the Daughters nationwide raised most of the Confederate monuments across the South, as well as the tall, rebel-topped pillar in Forest Lawn Cemetery and the striking "dying lion" sculpture at the old veterans home near Higginsville, Mo.

Setting aside nearby antebellum Lexington, the region's epicenter of Southern memory is surely Independence. Here meet the Civil War Roundtable of Western Missouri, the Civil War Study Group,

the Sons of Confederate Veterans and the Quantrill Society.

At a Sons meeting sat Patrick Cole, his eyes shaded by the blue-tinted spectacles favored by war re-enactors. With long brown hair and goatee, he seemed to walk off a page of antebellum history.

"Yes, ma'am," said Cole, 33, offering a genteel bow. "I'm a neo-Confederate and proud of it. I have lived under Federal domination all my life and believe the Southern government was the best form of governing America has ever seen."

But in a later interview, after Googling the hate-group-fighting Southern Poverty Law Center's definition of "neo-Confederate" — "a reactionary conservative ideology that ... overlaps with the views of white nationalists and other more radical extremist groups" — the Independence man recanted.

"I'm not that at all," he said. What ignited his interest in the Civil War was the history never learned in school. The details that keep emerging won't let go, he explained. What's more, his ability to "become" a Confederate soldier earned him a bit part in an upcoming movie, "Abraham Lincoln: Vampire Killer."

Although these lineage groups include FBI agents, police, firefighters and military veterans, many are mindful of a public who sees only a love for the Confederate flag and not their love for history.

Out-of-town hotels have denied the Daughters reservations, believing the group to be racist, Spencer said. Their display booth was vandalized at one.

The members shook their heads sadly as Sandi Leshikar recalled how her employer, just that day, jokingly "wanted to know when my Ku Klux Klan meeting would be over."

"It's frustrating," Spencer said. "Our number one goal is to remember our Southern roots.

"What's wrong with that?"

## VARIED VIEWPOINTS

Younger Americans might wonder, too.

Polled by Pew on the major reason the Civil War erupted, six out of every 10 people younger than 30 chose "states' rights."

But then, they didn't live through the racial turmoil of the mid-1900s.

When President Harry Truman desegregated the armed forces in 1948, South Carolina's Strom Thurmond founded the States' Rights Party and launched a presidential bid centered on racial separation.

The Ku Klux Klan and much of the Deep South waved the rebel flag as a symbol against federal efforts forcing states to integrate schools and giving voting rights to blacks.

Thurmond said nobody should "force the Southern people to break down segregation and admit the (black) race into our theaters, into our swimming pools, into our homes and into our churches."

For the next couple of decades, "states' rights certainly was code for segregation," said Washington University professor Wayne Fields, an expert on political rhetoric. "It has since become a softer, gentler term reflecting more of a Libertarian position. It's abstract, wrapped in an incredible amount of vagueness and ambiguity."

Many historians reject states' rights as the reason perhaps a quarter-million Southern men died. Espe-

cially since the Confederate constitution provided little in the way of additional states' rights than those outlined in the U.S. Constitution.

Both charters established a three-way central government — executive branch, Congress and Supreme Court. Both featured a "supremacy clause," enabling

---

*"You could say my family was bitter about that war. Still is."*

Jack Haley, Oak Grove

---

national legislation to reign over the states as the supreme law of the land.

One key difference: The Confederate constitution cited slaveholding as a specific right. States of the confederacy were not allowed the right to outlaw slavery.

When classroom teachers have the time to tackle the "slavery or states' rights" question — dates, battles

and who's who tend to eat up the hour — the safest answer is "both."

Historians agree that the institution of slavery was so vital to a Southern economy largely based on cotton — and crucial as well to emerging textile mills in the North — it drove the South to secede. Framers of the Confederacy considered secession their right.

Lincoln and Union men deemed the states' leaving to be unlawful, anarchic and treasonous, and they moved to block it. That, say Southern sympathizers, led to a needless bloodbath.

Even that pared-down explanation can create more arguments than some teachers care to encourage. But would it help or hurt young minds to ponder the words of Alexander H. Stephens, vice president of the Confederacy?

"Our new government is founded...its cornerstone rests," he said, "upon the great truth that the Negro is not equal to the white man: that slavery, subordination to the superior race, is his natural and normal condition."

Late in 2010, the conservative Texas Board of Education tried to change "slave trade" to "Atlantic triangular trade" in a new social studies textbook. It backed off, accepting "trans-Atlantic slave trade."

At Harvard, an argument goes on whether to honor at Memorial Hall the 71 graduates who fought for the South. Many are appalled at the idea, despite the fact that men who fought for Germany in World War II are remembered there.

Meanwhile, the Minneapolis park board was asked to change the name of Lake Calhoun because South Carolina Sen. John C. Calhoun was an outspoken ad-

**Jack Haley, of Oak Grove, overlooking the meadow where his great-grandfather stood and watched his world burn during the Civil War.** | RICH SUGG, THE KANSAS CITY STAR

A survey by Pew Research of 1,500 adults found that more than 50 percent say the Civil War is still relevant, most are indifferent when seeing a Confederate flag and almost half believe the war was mainly about state's rights and not slavery.

### Do you think the civil war is ...

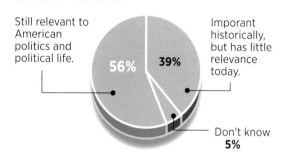

Still relevant to American politics and political life. **56%**

Imporant historically, but has little relevance today. **39%**

Don't know **5%**

### Your reaction when you see the Confederate flag displayed?

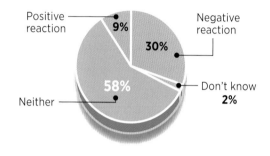

Positive reaction **9%**

Negative reaction **30%**

Neither **58%**

Don't know **2%**

### Your impression of the main cause of the Civil War?

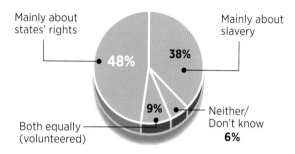

Mainly about states' rights **48%**

Mainly about slavery **38%**

Both equally (volunteered) **9%**

Neither/ Don't know **6%**

---

vocate of slavery in President Andrew Jackson's day.

The Abbeville Institute in South Carolina is named after Calhoun's birthplace. It's an intellectual sanctuary for more than 100 Dixie-devoted philosophers, authors, political scientists and law professors.

Its conferences were not broadly publicized until recent years, because of a feared backlash from academic peers.

Abbeville's critics at the Southern Poverty Law Center question the honesty of Abbeville's reason for being, as stated on the institute's Website by historian Eugene D. Genovese:

"Rarely these days, even on Southern campuses, is it possible to acknowledge the achievements of white people in the South."

Are George Washington and Thomas Jefferson really getting short shrift? Since when have William Faulkner, Tennessee Williams and Elvis been verboten in the classroom?

At Abbeville, founded in 2003 by Emory University philosopher Donald Livingston, the Civil War is called the "War to End Southern Independence."

While acknowledging slavery as an evil, Livingston contends it eventually would have vanished. White Americans are "scandalized, embarrassed by slavery... So, we don't want to talk about it."

The war's sesquicentennial would benefit from respectful dialogue from all sides, he said.

The Southern viewpoint "about a war fought on noble grounds prevailed for a century" until the civil-rights movement, said University of North Carolina historian David Goldfield: "What's happened since is the pendulum has swung all the way to the other side. Now we're depicting the North as a republic of virtue and the South as the evil empire."

And when charges of "evil" are thrown, he said, "all discussion ends."

### POISONOUS FEELINGS

Song lyrics tucked inside the program for the 11th Annual Confederate Heritage Dinner in Osceola, Mo., captured the mood of the room.

*Oh, I'm a good old rebel*
*Now that's just what I am*
*And for this Yankee nation*
*I do not give a damn...*

Sponsored by the Sons of Confederate Veterans, the dinner brought together 200 to remember what the hosts called the "War of Northern Aggression." Cars and trucks filled the parking lot; just as many had to park in the grass. Only two trucks sported rebel flags on bumpers, one captioned: "Fighting terrorism since 1861."

That was the year U.S. Sen./ Gen. Jim Lane and his Kansas Brigade came to Osceola, executed at least 10 local Southern men and reduced the thriving Osage River town to charred piles.

As the homemade rolls were cooling at the food tables, the ashes of that 150-year-old war crime still seemed warm. Not only were several Confederate flags on display, but also what Tony Horwitz in his bestseller "Confederates in the Attic" called "militant victimology"

The featured speaker, Paul Petersen, who had just published his third book on guerrilla William Quantrill, suggested that hype and misinformation still swirl around the 1863 massacre at Lawrence. The town was crawling with Yankee militants, making many of the 150-plus victims not so innocent, he said.

The raid became just more blasphemy of Quantrill's legacy by Yankee historians.

"No matter how many lives he saved or the property he protected" for the South, Petersen complained, "the Lawrence raid outweighs them all — that one, single instance."

Earlier, another speaker mentioned Union Gen. Nathaniel Lyon's death at Wilson's Creek, and the audience broke in applause.

*...Three hundred thousand Yankees*

*Is stiff in southern dust*
*We got three hundred thousand*
*Before they conquered us.*

In late 1861, a breakaway band of state legislators gathered in Neosho, Mo., and voted to secede. The Confederacy added a star to its flag, representing Missouri. But the Union ignored their action.

Under federal occupation and heavy-handed martial law, Missouri fast became a flaming mess. Residents had to swear a loyalty oath or face fines and/or imprisonment. Nearly 2,000 Missouri civilians were tried by military commission during the war — far more than in any other state.

Southern men, forced to join pro-Union militias, fled to the Confederate army or bushwhacker bands. Their capture often meant a death sentence, the same for any man caught feeding them or giving them information. Southern farmers were hanged in their barns, their women jailed and banished for pro-Southern remarks.

Both sections of the country had demonized the other, raising pre-war temperatures. The viperous feelings between Americans did not abate.

"The expedition to Lawrence was a gallant and perfectly fair blow at the enemy," rationalized the Examiner in Richmond, Va., "as the population of Kansas is malignant and scoundrelly beyond description."

After viewing the Confederate dead and captured at Westport in 1864, the pro-Union Kansas City Daily Journal of Western Commerce sniffed: "They seem to belong to a different race from ours, and most certainly to an inferior one. In truth, this war is one of intelligence, enlightened, and Christian civilization against barbarism."

*...I can't take up my musket*
*To fight 'em down no more*
*But I ain't a-goin' to love 'em.*
*Now that is certain sure.*

Given such bitter memories of Missouri Confederates, one might never know that twice as many Missouri volunteers joined the Union Army as fought for the South.

"Memory is an interesting thing," says Arnold Schofield, administrator of the Mine Creek Battlefield in Kansas.

"Missouri had pro-Southerners, but also a lot of pro-Union people, free blacks, even slave owners who wanted to remain in the Union — all these factions fighting each other....But in the memory of Missourians, it's easier to blame someone not from their state."

Back at the heritage dinner, some heaved blame at today's Washington. In Osceola, federal heavy-handedness still inflames.

Up stood a blue-jeaned, plaid-shirted man to speak his mind about the Obama administration: "Lee Harvey Oswald, where are you when we need you?"

His words seemed to hang over the all-white audience. Nobody applauded. Some groaned or rolled their eyes. Most stayed silent.

"We don't hate our country," said the embarrassed master of ceremonies. "We might not like where it's going, but we're here to honor our ancestors."

The Civil War ushered in the expansion of U.S. government's size and power, along with the income tax — begun under Lincoln to fund the war — and fresh grievances of how banks and industrial interests

**"This is a picture that talks!"** exclaimed Frank James upon viewing George Caleb Bingham's "Order No. 11." Probably the most significant painting to come out of the western theater of the Civil War, it depicts Kansas soldiers brutally forcing the evacuation of most of four Missouri border counties. Bingham, who was Missouri state treasurer at the time, protested in vain against Gen. Thomas Ewing's action and swore to use his oils against him in revenge. Two nearly identical large canvases depicting Ewing and his men were created in Independence after the war and used to try to ruin the general's political aspirations back in Ohio. | COURTESY OF THE STATE HISTORICAL SOCIETY OF MISSOURI

got preference over the little guy.

Across America, in states red and blue, "nullification" movements are springing up against an array of federal rules, especially health care reform.

So-called "tenthers" wield as their sword the 10th Amendment of the Bill of Rights: "The powers not delegated to the United States by the Constitution, nor prohibited by it to the States, are reserved to the States respectively, or to the people."

This clause is cited by Confederacy fans upholding the right of states to break away.

It's not just conservatives claiming the 10th. Californians want to use it to eliminate the federal government's prohibitions on pot possession. In other states, the gripes are aimed at federal gun laws, FDA rules applied to small dairy producers, or the executive branch using state National Guard troops in an undeclared war on terror.

"It's taken 150 years to get to the point we're at now," says Mike Maharrey of the Tenth Amendment Center, a California-based advocacy group. "It'll probably take another 150 years to get back to a limited government that the framers intended."

## REGIONAL DISDAIN

"Poor white trash," the frustrated Yankee occupiers labeled the Missouri insurgents they could not catch.

"Not one in a hundred could write," Lt. Col. Elias Caulkins of the 3rd Wisconsin alleged, inaccurately. "They are usually of a yellow sandy complexion … and they had uniformly bad teeth. …They were ignorant, uncombed, unwashed."

Such slander fed the flames of sectional disdain

then, but seems material for Jeff Foxworthy today.

"Rednecks," the comedian teases. You might be one "if more than one living relative is named after a Civil War general...If you are still holding on to Confederate money because you think the South will rise again."

Steven Heiner seems to defy all the labels.

Born in Singapore, Asian in appearance and staunchly Catholic (with no known family links to the war). Still, he says:

"I consider myself a Southern partisan."

He arrived in Texas with his parents at age 9. He fell in love with football, country music, conservative politics and fried chicken. The books of Faulkner and Flannery O'Connor stirred a romance for the Old South.

"Spanish moss hanging on large trees in South Carolina, Fort Sumter in the distance, yeah, you can say that conjures up some special feelings — a connectedness to a gone-away world," says Heiner, 32, who runs a Kansas City company that prepares students for college entrance exams.

When he was a student himself — English Literature at Rockhurst University — Heiner attended a summer session at Abbeville.

"I would not call myself a neo-Confederate for the same reason I would not fly a Confederate flag outside my house, north of the Mason-Dixon line. It carries too much baggage for an American populace thick on emotion and thin on cogitation."

To Gwen Grant, the flag represents nothing good.

"It's the same as seeing a swastika," said Grant, executive director of the Urban League of Greater Kansas City. "It conjures up, for me, all the negative history of our country, and not all that I love about America...

"What exactly are they celebrating? It only reminds us of the struggle black Americans and whites had to endure."

---

*"I'm not ashamed of my Southern heritage. It's who I am, my family's history"*

Kurt Holland, Missouri City

---

To Kurt Holland the Confederate flag is a reverent symbol. A way to both honor and remember the dead.

At his Missouri City home, he unfolds, then shakes open the red cotton material with its blue cross and 13 bold stars. As big as a full-sized bed quilt, with tiny hand-stitching, it is his most prized possession.

"This isn't from China," he says softly, fingers tracing the outline of one of the stars.

This flag once draped the coffin of his great-great-grandfather, Thomas C. Holland, a captain in Company G, 28th Virginia Infantry. At Gettysburg, he was shot in the jaw and left among the dead. He survived a prisoner of war camp and spent the next 60 years mostly in Kansas City, where he was active in the United Confederate Veterans.

Holland, 50, flies another, newer nylon version of the rebel flag on Confederate holidays — and always on July 3rd, when his great-great-grandfather rushed with Pickett's division against the Union center on Cemetery Ridge.

"I'm not ashamed of my Southern heritage," Holland said with a shrug. "It's who I am, my family's history.

"I fly the U.S. flag, too."

He walks over to a shelf and pulls out a folded flag in a triangular glass-enclosed case.

"This one came from my stepfather's funeral. He was a World War II veteran... And I'm pretty proud of him, too."

Holland is also a member of the Sons. He says he rejects political correctness and will push back against those who twist Southern history. "I'm angry with those hate groups who have taken over our flag," he said. "That's not what we're about."

That's why, too, he doesn't paste Confederate flags on his truck's bumper. It's disrespectful.

"When I fly my Confederate flag, it is my freedom of expression. I think about all the brave men who put their lives on the line for what they believed...

"Their states' sovereignty."

# 150 YEARS LATER, FLAG CAN STIR EMOTIONS

By **LEE HILL KAVANAUGH** ★ THE KANSAS CITY STAR

HIGGINSVILLE, Mo. | Few would have noticed one less rebel battle flag here.

In the 2011 memorial ceremonies for the Jefferson Davis birthday, a sea of red and blue fluttered across the 837 graves of soldiers, guerrillas and their wives.

A half-dozen more ringed the copy of the Dying Lion of Lucerne, a marble ode to the Lost Cause.

But one was absent.

What was once the most controversial flag in Missouri could not be found in any glass display case inside the chapel.

When asked where it was, state parks workers headed for the basement. In a storage area near a water tank, a colored wad was spotted in a floor cubby — a U.S. flag.

"I'm sure this one is waiting to be burned," said an embarrassed official, moving it off the floor.

On a shelf in another room were several boxes, including one with a handwritten note: "Confederate flag taken down ca. 2000."

"The wrong date, a mistake," said the official.

The rebel banner was the last to officially fly over the old bones interred here. A flap over a similar flag a half-continent away brought it down in January 2003.

Every four years, the rebel flag at the South Carolina State House had been a litmus test for presidential candidates in that state's early primary.

In 2000, the flag shifted from over the dome to a Confederate war memorial on the Capitol grounds. But the state's black citizens, Democrats mostly, wanted the hated symbol of bondage and racism gone.

In 2003, when Rep. Dick Gephardt ran for president, it was his turn to take the test. Take it down, answered the Missouri Democrat. Shouldn't be flown "any time, anywhere."

Of course, back in his home state, it was fluttering here at the cemetery, as well as at the Fort Davidson Historic Site near Pilot Knob — a fact Gephardt quickly learned from journalists.

Calls were made. The flags came down. Even the pole in the graveyard came down to eliminate temptation.

To critics, it all seemed to wave a white flag — to political correctness.

Why could not a Confederate flag honor Confederate dead at a Confederate cemetery? Think of history, they said. Remember tradition.

Except, newspaper articles from the last two centuries reported that only Old Glory flew over the grounds when this was a home for Confederate veterans. The rebel flag came out when the coffin of each was draped with it.

In 1950, after taps was played over the last old soldier, the Confederate Home of Missouri closed. Grass went unmowed. Buildings fell into disrepair.

Not until the early 1980s, when the state created a park and historical site, did the rebel flag whip in the Missouri breezes, this time beneath the national and state flags.

Rebel flag displays in other states have not been so innocent. The all-white South Carolina legislature defiantly raised theirs above the State House during the civil rights era.

Georgia decided — after the Brown v. Topeka desegregation case — that its new state flag should be the Confederate "Southern Cross" — the same

A variety of flags fluttered at Confederate Memorial Day ceremonies at the Confederate Memorial State Historic Site outside Higginsville, Mo. Honoring ancestors, guests laid flowers on the cemetery monument.

| KEITH MYERS,
THE KANSAS CITY STAR

Virginia battle flag often seen on bumpers, T-shirts and tattoos.

By 2003, that flag's design was changed again to the less recognizable first Confederate flag known as the "Stars and Bars."

Mississippi today has the only state flag incorporating the Southern Cross. Adopted in the late 19th century, nearly two-thirds voted to keep it in a 2001 referendum.

The rebel flag at Higginsville was never that kind of a political statement, said Kay Russell, who recently retired as the park's interpretive resource specialist.

"When the flagpole was out in the cemetery, and we flew it over the veterans who were buried out there, I felt it was right."

Time passed. Quietly, the policy softened.

"We have to ask special permission from the governor's office whenever we want to fly the flag here, so that's what we do," said Dawson Heathman, with the Confederate Memorial Friends Association. "We jump through their hoops."

The confederate flag's removal was heartbreaking, he said. "They're trying to change history."

# GALLERY OF LOCAL GUERRILLAS

This display of "bushmen" is made possible, courtesy of National Park Service, Collection of Wilson's Creek National Battlefield (WCNB); State Historical Society of Missouri, Columbia (SHS); Missouri Valley Room, Kansas City Library (MVR); the Collection of Emory A. Cantey, Jr.; Quantrillsguerrillas.com. (CC); Lone Jack Civil War Battlefield Museum (LJBM).

**▲ James Liddell**
Rode with William Quantrill; supposedly was at the Centralia, Mo., massacre, later one of the James gang. (WCNB)

**Clark Hockensmith ▶**
Went with Quantrill to Kentucky, where he was gunned down trying to save his mortally wounded chief. (WCNB)

**◄ Archie Clement** (left); **Dave Pool; Bill Hendricks**
Among Bloody Bill Anderson's killers, Little Archie probably did the most scalping, throat cutting and beheading. Pool, who rode with George Todd, had a thing for killing the "damned Dutch," that is, German immigrants. Hendricks was wintering in Texas in December 1863 when they went to Gabe's Picture Gallery in Sherman. After posing, the story goes, the guerrillas threw Gabe and his equipment out a second-story window into the street. (SHS)

**George Todd ▲**
This Kansas City stonemason's son overthrew Quantrill in spring 1864 card game; died fighting for Gen. Sterling Price outside Independence. (MVR)

**▲ William Anderson**
Sobriquet "Bloody Bill," given after the war, was truly earned when he had nearly two dozen furloughed and unarmed Union soldiers pulled off a train at Centralia and slaughtered. (SHS)

**▲ Jeremiah "Vard" Cockrell** A rebel recruiter and commander at Lone Jack; older brother to CSA Gen. Francis Cockrell, who led the famed 1st Missouri Brigade. (WCNB)

**John S. Nichols ▶**
Posing shortly before hanging in 1863, he promised to show Yankees how a Southern man dies. (Note the guard's pistol caught in the image.) (WCNB)

GRAPHIC BY DARRYL LEVINGS AND NEIL NAKAHODO | THE KANSAS CITY STAR

**John Jarrette ▶**

One of Quantrill's band during the war; rode with the James gang after. (WCNB)

**▼ George Maddox**

The only one tried for Lawrence raid, but a venue change, and probably jury bribes, got him acquitted. (WCNB)

**◀ John McCorkle** (left) and **T.B. Harris**

McCorkle would live to write the best guerrilla memoir about his guerrilla days. Harris was his brother-in-law. Both had women kin in the Kansas City prison collapse; both rode with Quantrill. (WCNB)

**▼ William A. Brown, Greenbury Austin, Thomas H. Brown**

Local recruits who fought at Lone Jack under Col. Upton Hays, another former freighter turned rebel. (LJBM)

**◀ Fletch Taylor, Frank James** (seated), **Jesse James**

Taylor led a band including the James boys until losing his arm in 1864. Frank, said to carry Shakespeare in his saddle bags, rode some with Todd later. Jesse, recovering from a bullet in the chest at age 17, gravitated toward Anderson. (SHS)

**▲ Riley Crawford**

Given at age 15 by his mother to Quantrill to avenge murder of his father and burning of family home near Blue Springs by 5th Missouri State Militia. (CC)

**◀ Dick Yager**

Former Jackson County freighter used trail experience to raid all the way to Council Grove, Kan.; minié ball to the head ended his career in 1864 at Arrow Rock. (SHS)

# Mystery surrounds five Kansas City deaths

By **DARRYL LEVINGS** ★ THE KANSAS CITY STAR

The screams of frightened women carried up and down Grand Avenue. Then, as passers-by turned and stared, two buildings collapsed in a crunch of brick and a cloud of plaster dust.

Minutes later, soldiers and civilians, some swearing, all sweating in the August heat, tore at broken beams, trying to extract the prisoners from the rubble.

Teenage girls, weeping from broken limbs and dangerous cuts, were pulled out. A crowd gathered, many angrily gesturing at the four bodies laid nearby.

No accident, some muttered. The Yankees did it.

As conspiracy theories go, this one had legs. The victims were Southern women, kin to notorious bushwhackers.

Josephine, 15, little sister to William Anderson — a man whom it was unwise to anger — perished in the Aug. 13, 1863, collapse. Another victim was Charity Kerr, whose brother, John McCorkle, would say:

"We could stand no more."

Days later, they and hundreds more galloped

**Harper's Weekly's 1861 version of Federal soldiers searching the home of rebelious Southern women for incriminating weapons and letters.** | COURTESY OF THE MISSOURI VALLLEY ROOM, KANSAS CITY PUBLIC LIBRARY

through the streets of Lawrence, getting their revenge on the male citizens of that unlucky town, although historians agree William Clarke Quantrill had been planning his raid well before the jail disaster.

But the mystery lingers: Why did No. 13 on Grand fall?

One clue leads to the cellar.

Federal authorities had been arresting Southern women to eliminate the material and moral support they offered to bushwhackers.

Some got released; more often they were shipped off to the large Gratiot Street Prison in St. Louis and banished from the state with little more than the clothes on their backs.

A dozen or so ended up lodging on the second floor of the No. 13, better known as the Thomas Building. It was just south of what today is the Sprint Center.

The first floor was a Jewish grocery. The third level apparently was empty. That floor had been added for a studio by artist George Caleb Bingham, who possessed the property.

That cellar? Be patient.

Paul Petersen, author of three books on Quantrill, agrees with the old talk that vengeful Yankees "premeditated their designs" of sabotage.

While few go that far, it appears that Gen. Thomas Ewing, headquartered in Kansas City, had been made aware of the deterioration at No. 13, but did not act on it.

Bingham, a strong Union man but one who hated Ewing's guts, vainly sought federal reimbursement, claiming his building was "destroyed while thus oc-cupied, by the act of soldiers in removing columns."

While Southerners saw a dastardly plot, Federals groped for other theories. Many histories contend the structure was dilapidated — although it was built in the late1850s — and victim to a gust of wind. Other folks blamed hogs rooting around the foundation.

As late as 1910, Kansas historian William E. Connelley was still writing how the women brought their fate down upon themselves by digging through the foundation. How they would dig out from a second floor was not explained.

What is obvious is the key role of the smaller Cockrell Building used as a guardhouse next door. It likely collapsed first, bringing down the Thomas Building with it.

That the Thomas Building was stressed is clear. Cracks appeared in walls and ceilings. The worried merchant had removed much of his stock.

Now, it's time to descend into that cellar.

Eleven years after the disaster, Dr. Joshua Thorne, the Union surgeon responsible for the medical needs of the prisoners, came forward.

While the second floor housed gentile Southern ladies, he testified, the cellar held women "of bad character and diseased."

To soldiers barracksed next door, however, it was a harem only a few bricks away. Thorne said they tore out large holes in the common cellar wall, weakening the buildings above.

Edward Leslie, in his 1996 book about Quantrill — "The Devil Knows How to Ride" — slyly called the theory of the prostitutes "as natural as a sudden gust of wind." Bruce Nichols, finishing his third volume of "Guerrilla Warfare in Civil War Missouri," finds that theory more likely than any plot to kill the women.

Petersen, however, contends that Thorne had changed his story. His book, "Quantrill of Missouri: The Making of a Guerrilla Warrior," refers to Mattie Lykins, wife of a former mayor, who quoted the doctor at the scene that day as saying:

"Not a blue coat will be found (in the debris); every man who has been detailed to stand guard at this prison for the last few days and weeks knew the house to be unsafe and have kept themselves at a safe distance from the trembling walls. I knew the building to be unsafe and notified the military authorities of the fact, and suggested the removal of the women prisoners, but my suggestion was not heeded and before you is the result."

If true, that hardly proves murder. Lykins, an outspoken cousin of Confederate Lt. Gen. Thomas "Stonewall" Jackson, soon was banished herself.

While the soldiers did chop away at the cellar's supporting brickwork, Petersen said, no women were down there.

Charlie Harris, who researched all of this for the Missouri Historical Review, also discounts the hookers-below theory. Too dark and dank, reasoned the Wichita lawyer, related to three women in the collapse.

"You couldn't keep people down there for any length of time." Besides, he argued, why would the soldiers go to the trouble of digging through? "They'd just walk around."

The soldiers removed structural supports in the Cockrell Building simply to enlarge a first-floor common area, he believes.

No dastardly plot at all.

"If you were going to kill these girls," Harris asked, "wouldn't you do it in a little more efficient manner rather to bring down a building and hope it causes the other building to fall, too?"

While the conflict in the Kansas City region was exceedingly personal and violent, physical harm to women was rare. The war occurred during the Victorian era, and many combatants adopted a chivalric code of sorts. Only one black woman may have died in the Lawrence raid, Cole Younger said, shot by accident.

To that, Petersen notes the rising fury of Kansas soldiers that summer. Just in June, George Todd's band killed 16 troopers of the 9th Kansas Cavalry in an ambush on the Fort Scott Road (today's Wornall Road) south of Westport.

"They wanted retaliation," he said in an interview, "but the Kansans couldn't take it out on the guerrillas because they couldn't catch them."

But the jailed women, bushwhacker family, were handy.

Not all were girls, as many say: Charity McCorkle Kerr was 32.

Armenia Crawford Selvey and Susan Crawford Whitsett Vandever were both married and in their late 20s. They were not twins, as some histories report.

Their brother was Riley Crawford, one of the youngest members of Quantrill's band in 1863. Cole Younger was a cousin. The sisters had been arrested on a trip to Kansas City to buy flour and cloth, allegedly destined for guerrillas.

Anderson's sisters were young: Mary, known as Molly, was 18; Josephine, probably15; and Martha, called Mattie or Jenny, just 13.

Harris found one report that alleged they were caught with percussion caps for firearms.

Seeming determined to spoil all the good tales, Harris also does not believe reports that irritated Union jailers had chained a 12-pound ball to Martha's ankle. She suffered two broken legs in the disaster, but it was Mary who was "crippled for life."

Charity Kerr's widowed sister-in-law, "Nannie" Harris McCorkle, either 19 or 20, managed to leap out a window.

The bodies of the Crawford women and McCorkle's sister were taken to the small Davis-Smith Cemetery beyond the village of Raytown.

"I was a girl of eleven at the time as I remember that the Union men sent three caskets containing my cousins to Little Blue," Eliza Harris later would write. "With the caskets was the satchel of trinkets and dry goods that my sister and Charity had gone to town to buy."

Their resting place, now on private property between the lanes of Missouri 350 east of Westridge Road, is overgrown with weeds. Local historians hope to mark it in some way.

Josephine Anderson is buried in Union Cemetery, not far south of the grave of Bingham.

Yet there's another mystery. Who was the fifth victim, a "Mrs. Wilson," who lingered a spell before dying?

A Union spy, some think, placed to eavesdrop on the women; a Mrs. Wilson had tried to warn Federals before they were surprised in the 1862 Battle of Independence.

Women spies were not unheard of in the West. One was Elizabeth W. Stiles, whose husband reportedly was killed Oct. 15, 1862, in Todd's raid on Shawneetown. Afterward, Federal records showed her employed "as a Spy & Secret Agent on this border."

Todd had his own spy, but she wasn't as effective as Stiles. Arrested trying to get a pass to leave Independence, a Miss Eliza Brown confessed, "that she was sent in by Capt. Todd to ascertain if possible the number of our forces then in town with the promise if she did so, he would make her a present of some fine dresses."

Connelley wrote of another young woman, Alice Van Ness, who escaped injury in the collapse.

She was a favorite among her Union captors for her singing voice. Lt. Cyrus Leland Jr. was such a friend that he arranged to have her banished — so she could join a passing theatrical company and start a fine career away from the war.

The surviving Anderson sisters? Less popular, a year later, they were arrested again, sent to St. Louis, placed on a steamboat and dumped in Arkansas.

# Keeping her family tree alive

By LEE HILL KAVANAUGH ★ THE KANSAS CITY STAR

**GENERATIONS**
**A series of family memories about local ancestors in the Civil War.**

She brings out the photo. A sepia image of a man from 1864 stares back. James "Jim Crow" Chiles, in his early 30s, hat at a jaunty angle, bears a resemblance to actor Johnny Depp.

"See how handsome he was?" sighs Joanne Chiles Eakin, her fingers caressing the image. "I've always said he could park his boots under my bed anytime."

And the 76-year-old chuckles at her wickedness — especially because Chiles was kin, and murderous kin at that. Still, she says, "He was the one who started it all for me."

Eakin has dug out hundreds of tales about her 30 to 40 relatives who lived in Jackson County in the 1800s. Many fought in the Civil War. But it was this black sheep of a cousin who, in 1958, ignited her lifelong love affair with the era.

Because of Jim Crow, she ventured into archives and libraries to pore over musty newspaper clippings piecing together his life, his personality, his story.

Such as, why the nickname? "He was the most agile dancer of the Jim Crow polka than anyone in Jackson County."

Eakin had found a copy of the sheet music a few years earlier.

During this romance, she put together 46 books

Each year, Joanne Chiles Eakin, editor of "The Blue & Grey Chronicle," puts a Confederate flag on the grave of her ancestor, James "Jim Crow" Chiles in Wood-lawn Cemetery in Independence. Jim Crow's story inspired Eakin's lifelong love affair with the Civil War. | KEITH MYERS, THE KANSAS CITY STAR

from Civil War records and genealogies, another dozen as a co-author.

Jim Crow got her invites for coffee and conversation with his nephew, Harry Truman.

In a sense, Jim Crow also introduced her to a well-known Hollywood producer, who called her up one day, asking for her expertise for his movie, "Ride With the Devil."

"Ang Lee and I talked," is all Eakin will say of her work on the sets. "I made sure he knew you couldn't be neutral and live in Jackson County. The war affected everybody."

One of the main characters in the film, a dashing young guerrilla from a good family, is Jack Bull Chiles.

"Jack Bull is Jim Crow," confides Eakin, who also has chatted with author Daniel Woodrell, who altered several names in his book, "Woe to Live On."

In the real-life drama, Chiles did some riding with William Quantrill, but ended up with Gen. Joe Shelby, she said. Her direct ancestor, Henry Clay Chiles, a western freighter, was not a combatant in the war.

On a wall of Eakin's home is a rendering of an aerial view of the City of Independence in 1861, the year the war began. She peers at the tiny drawings of buildings. She shows where slaves were sold, where men waged war in the streets and where in 1873, Jim Crow breathed his last.

"It was a bullet in his back, right in the Independence Square," Eakin said. "That cowardly Peacock shot him in the back while Peacock's son held his arms down."

That's her version. There are others. She shakes her head.

> *"Ang Lee and I talked," is all Eakin will say of her work on the sets. "I made sure he knew you couldn't be neutral and live in Jackson County. The war affected everybody."*

"The really sad part is what happened to Jim Crow's son."

But this is not the time or place to tell that story, she says. That will come later.

Here, it should be noted: Chiles was not a model citizen, having killed a lawyer in the Noland Hotel in 1859 for remarking on his poor table manners. He was acquitted, perhaps due in part to his family's standing or money.

After the war, he owned a livery stable in Independence, where he had a reputation as a horseman. In Kansas City, he ran a gambling house and saloon, "Headquarters," where he fed his image as a bad man.

"One-man reign of terror," David McCullough wrote in his Truman biography.

Eakin knows McCullough, too. "I knew he was going to slander Jim Crow. He had a hatred of him. Why else do you think I'd refuse to let him have that picture that he wanted so desperately?"

But even a colleague of Jim Crow who called him kind and considerate noted how he was "subject to violent fits of anger, and when angry, a very dangerous man."

McCullough and others said Jim Crow had a penchant for whipping or shooting black men, including one in 1869. But Eakin notes that the family slaves chose to stay with the Chiles after the war. They're there in the 1870 census.

Eakin combs microfilm from the National Archives on her own reader and then pours the old stories into her bi-monthly, "The Blue & Grey Chronicle." Her collections from the past are her gift to the future.

A former president of the United Daughters of the Confederacy and the Heart of America Genealogical Society, she belongs to a dozen history groups. She worries that no one else in her family cares much about the Civil War era and their ancestors' stories.

The bedrooms of her ranch house are filled with boxes of notes, papers and books. An entire wall with a fireplace was built with bricks from the property of a home burned under General Order No. 11.

Another story she tells is about her grandmother, another "ever so great" relative, a term she uses to skip around counting up all the "greats."

Surprised one afternoon by a group of Yankees on horseback, she says, "they demanded her to fix them dinner, so she did. But when the men were done, one officer leaned way back in his chair and said with a grin on his face and all mean-like, 'I just shot your son in yonder woods.'"

But she knew it wasn't true, Eakin goes on. The son was in Texas. "Later on, she learned it was her nephew, though. Those Yankees were mean.

"...And after the war, you couldn't just move back. You had to prove you owned the property. But how could you prove that when the Yankees burned everything down?"

Which leads Eakin into another tale about another relative, John P. Webb, of Oak Grove. Webb was rich from the California gold rush, she says, but returned to Jackson County after the war. On the Independence courthouse steps, as the properties of his friends were sold, he bought them up.

**James "Jim Crow" Chiles in captured Union garb in 1864.**

"He gave them their land back," she says, "even if the owner couldn't pay him. I'm very proud of him."

For at least 30 years, she guesses, Eakin planted rebel flags on Oak Grove and Lone Jack graves of ancestors on Decoration Day.

"It was Decoration Day years before the government decided to change it to Memorial Day," she explains, disgusted.

She always ends up at Woodlawn in Independence, her last stop the Chiles family marker.

Which is where she is now, under the shade of a century-old tree. "Now, I'll tell you what happened," she begins:

The Saturday night before Jim Crow died, his daughter's pony and several of his thoroughbreds were poisoned. He went into town to see if he could find out who did it.

Elijah, 12, went after him and saw Deputy Marshall James Peacock shoot his father as another man held Jim Crow's arms tight.

Why did they fight? Some say Chiles was drunk and slapped Peacock. Others say Peacock had a grudge against Chiles because he got away with the 1869 killing of a black man. McCullough described Peacock as having the grit to duel.

Eakin refers to an old newspaper obituary for her telling of the story. In the melee, Elijah, half blind but brave, caught a bullet, too. The boy was carried to a nearby hotel, where he lingered for two days — and apologized to kin for not saving his father, Jim Crow Chiles. She sighs once more.

"When I first read that it made me cry....So sad."

# Primary sources offer insight on war's cause

So, which is it: Slavery or states' rights? One would think that 15 decades after the firing on Fort Sumter, we would have gotten closer to answering the question of what caused the South to secede.

Yet, the public debate continues to rage.

Newspapers, Web pages, the airwaves and barrooms will be filled with arguments over this fundamental question.

But much of this will be based on wishful thinking, not primary documents of the day.

Rarely, in our rush to define the nature of secession, do we ask the secessionists what they thought they were doing.

After all, secession was debated at length following Abraham Lincoln's election in the autumn of 1860. The paper trail stretches more than 8,000 pages.

The political wrangling filled the halls of Congress,

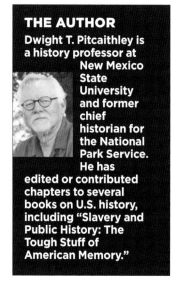

**THE AUTHOR**
Dwight T. Pitcaithley is a history professor at New Mexico State University and former chief historian for the National Park Service. He has edited or contributed chapters to several books on U.S. history, including "Slavery and Public History: The Tough Stuff of American Memory."

11 state secession conventions and the general assemblies of Tennessee and Kentucky.

The proceedings from these frenzied arenas were published with a sense of urgency.

It was indeed a national drama, one that left many observations by those with key roles:

"The question of Slavery is the rock upon which the Old Government split: it is the cause of secession," pronounced one delegate from Alabama's convention.

A senator from Mississippi argued: "We claim that there is property in slaves, and they deny it. Until we shall settle, upon some basis, that point of controversy, it is idle to talk of going any further."

A delegate to Virginia's convention declared: "Sir, the great question which is now uprooting this Government to its foundation — the great question which underlies all our deliberations here, is the question of African slavery."

By the time of Lincoln's victory in November 1860, white Southerners had convinced themselves that Lincoln was an abolitionist and that as soon as he took office on March 4, 1861, the curtain would come down on the South's economic engine — slavery.

As one delegate to South Carolina's convention asserted, the Palmetto State "first felt the blow inflicted by the election of an enemy to Southern institutions, elected by Abolition States upon Abolition issues."

Missouri's Trusten Polk was more specific. What could the slave-holding states expect, he lectured the U.S. Senate following the Republican victory, "but that all the patronage and all the power of the Federal Government, in all its departments, would be brought to bear upon the institution of slavery in the South, in order to compass its destruction?"

The formal declarations of secession from South Carolina, Georgia, Mississippi and Texas all announced that Republican threats to slavery prompted their leaving.

Mississippi's convention put it most emphatically. "Our position is thoroughly identified with the institution of slavery — the greatest material interest of the world ... and a blow at slavery is a blow at commerce and civilization."

With Lincoln heading to the White House, "There was no choice left us but submission to the mandates of abolition, or a dissolution of the Union, whose principles had been subverted to work out our ruin."

While Polk believed the victory of the "abolitionists" in 1860 was reason enough for the state to secede, Rep. John Richard Barret, a fellow Missourian, was of a different mind.

Agreeing that Republicans were abolitionists by a different name, Barret argued strongly against disunion suggesting that "while it may bring upon the country the direst of all calamities, it is a remedy for no evil, real or imaginary."

The 104 delegates to the Missouri's secession convention tended to favor Barret's view of the situation over Polk's.

Like Barret, they tended to believed the institution of slavery actually was better protected under the Constitution of the United States than under some other compact.

As Sample Orr, a delegate from Green County, argued practically that, "The only salvation for the institution of slavery is her adherence to the Government that protects slavery. Now, if they (fugitive slaves) go to Illinois, we get some of them back; but in the case of secession, we get none."

Since the acquisition of the Mexican Cession in 1848, Congress had debated the issue of slavery in Western territories.

It formed much of the Compromise of 1850, echoed throughout the Kansas-Nebraska controversy, was decided — or so many thought — by the Supreme Court's 1857 Dred Scott decision, became the center of the Lincoln-Douglas debates and marked the pivot upon which the election of 1860 turned.

M.L. Linton, representing St. Louis, thought the extension of slavery into the West was a spurious argument. The desert West was completely unsuited for the institution.

"The South desires to be permitted to do what she would not do if permitted, namely, to carry slavery into Territories unfitted for it. What a cause to fight for and to bleed for — a war for the extension of slavery where it could not exist!"

Abram Comingo of Independence agreed.

"There is no disguising the fact," he asserted, "that unless this question is adjusted in a satisfactory manner, civil war will ensue, as well as a total dissolution and disruption."

Ultimately, the delegates to Missouri's convention agreed with Uriel Wright from St. Louis that "if secession is right, there can never be any government on earth. Our Government will be the last, if secession be right."

They also understood that while Republicans had won the executive branch, Democrats had won the congressional elections of 1860 and would control both houses of Congress for the next two years.

In addition, the judicial branch remained firmly in the control of Roger B. Taney, the pro-slavery chief justice of the Supreme Court.

Unlike the states of the Deep South, Missouri opted for reason over passion.

Missouri's secession convention deliberated for three weeks and confronted the same issues and perceived threats to slavery that prompted 11 other states to secede.

At the end of the day, however, they determined that the election of an anti-slavery Republican president was not sufficient cause for disunion.

On March 19, 1861, with only one dissenting vote, the delegates agreed that "there is no adequate cause to impel Missouri to dissolve her connection with the Federal Union, but on the contrary she will labor for such an adjustment of existing troubles as will secure the peace as well as the rights and equality of all the States."

A FAMILY LETTER:

# 'SISTER I AM GLAD I AM A REBBLE'

*On June 27, 1864, John Thailkill wrote his sister, Nancy Stanton, from Andrew County to explain that he would never take the oath of allegience to the United States. He had just escaped after a month of hard labor in a prison stone quarry at Alton, Ill., a "federal bastiel." Records showed he added insult to injury by stealing the guard's gun. The rebel captain had been captured while recruiting north of the Missouri River for Maj. Gen. Sterling Price's army in Arkansas. He did not head straight south as he told his sister, however. Instead, the former Holt County painter became a guerrilla chieftain, his band playing a role in the "Paw Paw" rebellion in Platte County in July, the plunder of Kingston, the surrender of the Keytesville militia garrison, the destruction of a Federal supply train near Rocheport and the slaughter of nearly 100 Union infantrymen at the Battle of Centralia. Thailkill may have joined Price and Gen. Jo Shelby in their march toward the Battle of Westport; he was with those Missouri Confederates who went to Mexico the next spring rather than surrender. Unlike the others, he never returned to his "glories country."*

Dear Sister

You may think it strange that I have not wrote to you before this time but I have been trying so hard to keep from being captured again. I maid my escape on the 10th of this month and have been a free man since, o sister you cannot imagine the pleasure that it is to me to once more be out of the hands of the tyrents Dear Sister you cannot imagine how badley I was treated whilst in the federal bastiel ... Sister you wanted me to take the oath and come home as dearley as I love you all I would rather never See you then to take this oath one that would force me to support a abolitionis government one that I do so biterly detest No Dear sister I Should stand to be shot twenty times before I would take it had I not made my escape I think I would have died in prison ... Sister I am glad I am a rebble you do not know how disgraceful your party has acted in our glories country dixie but there is a time when we will have the pleasure of pointing out to them ther errers Sister when we shall have gained our indipendence which I am sertain we will we will have a Glories country one of the richest and best governments in the world o sister, the people of the south are so kind so Noble and so brave the Northern hords have tryed to whip us back to live with them this they can not do we will dye to a man first they feds have had 5 to 1 and then can not whip us now they are trying to whip us with Negroes of the south, your party says they are fighting for the consitution of ther country this is not so the negro is the property of the south by the constution of the united states of Amarica and they are instead of protectin them and ther rits they are steeling them and other property if you could see our once beautiful country now laid a wast you would not blaim me for being in the rebel ranks No Dear sister I am not ashaime to say that I am a rebble and if I am shot in the defence of my country o will dy in a glories cause... before you get this I will be with my Brothers in armes in the south this is the last letter I will write to any of you untill this war is over I start for General Pries this evening if I have no bad luck I will reach him in 10 days give all my brothers and sisters my best Love....I remain your effectionate Brother John Thrailkill.

| COURTESY OF JAMES W. FARLEY,
CO-AUTHOR OF MISSOURIEBELS REMEMBERED:
SI GORDON & JOHN THAILKILL

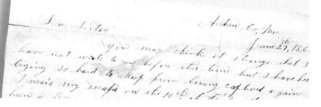

Part 4

The Civil War and today's military

# Terror's lessons

The hostilities of 150 years ago along the Kansas-Missouri line hold valuable insights for American soldiers serving in Iraq and Afghanistan

By **BRIAN BURNES** ★ THE KANSAS CITY STAR

L EAVENWORTH | A more fitting place for Army officers to come and study insurgencies and counterguerrilla tactics would be hard to find in the United States.

For it was from right here that Union soldiers ventured out to butt heads with the bushwackers who ruled the nearby Missouri countryside.

Proud of its part in taming the West, Fort Leavenworth offers little evidence, beyond some old graves in the cemetery, of its history in the bloody suppression of revolt next door. No displays about "jayhawkers" or "Red Legs" are in the post museum; no statues of their commanders are to be found. But in the class-

## HOW THE WAR INFLUENCED TODAY'S CULTURE

The emergence of cameras and the telegraph brought the war home more quickly than ever before.

Baseball became America's pastime when soldiers on both sides began playing the game.

The legends of Jesse James and other Missouri bushwhackers-turned-bandits still hold power in Hollywood.

rooms at the U.S. Army Command and General Staff College, chapters of the Civil War are remembered, 150-year-old lessons even taught. Not so much Gettysburg or Chancellorville, either, but of places mostly unheard of back east — bloody places, such as Grinter's farm, Baxter Springs, Centralia, Lawrence.

In an era of prowling Predator drones, it may seem strange that anything would carry over from the days of black powder, but the past has a way of circling around to surprise us on many fronts, cultural as well as military.

The old war still sneaks into our language: "Shoddy" comes from substandard material used in some Federal uniforms; "deadline" comes quite literally from the specific distance a prisoner of war could venture out before being shot by a guard.

It affected what holidays we observe and how. Even Santa Claus, as we know him today, first showed up in 1862 with gifts for Union soldiers.

Faced with more than 600,000 dead by war's end — today's population percentage equivalent would be 6 million — American attitudes toward death underwent wrenching change. The war prompted the invention of national cemeteries and military pensions. Modern funeral practices evolved from the desire to ship home and view one last time the physical remains of a soldier son or husband.

The thousands of crude battlefield amputations likewise led to a new industry in improved prosthetics, somewhat like the high-tech revolution in artificial limbs that has followed from the IED-strewn roads of Iraq and Afghanistan.

But perhaps the loudest echoes seem from our own bitter Missouri-Kansas border stories, where civilians

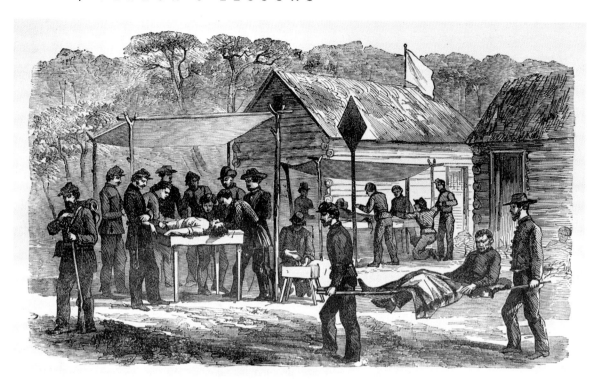

Civil War surgeons preferred outdoor field hospitals, the better for light and the dispersal of chloroform fumes. The Union Army began the war with 113 surgeons and ended with 12,000 having served. The Confederacy had about 3,200. | MISSOURI VALLEY ROOM, KANSAS CITY PUBLIC LIBRARY

were gunned down by fanatics on both sides and sorties into the hostile countryside often meant ambush, where surrender often was not recognized and atrocities with knives not uncommon.

"I get emails from former students in Iraq and Afghanistan who tell me how they see a lot of similarities between Bloody Kansas and where they are," said Terry Beckenbaugh, an assistant military history professor at Leavenworth's U.S. Army Command and General Staff College.

At the college, where officers returning from Iraq and

Afghanistan enroll in the 10-month course at what is considered the Army's grad school, all take H100, "The Western Way of War." The dozen two-hour lessons cover from about 1400 through the end of World War I.

The Civil War gets just two hours, but Ethan Rafuse, military history professor added: "Part of my pitch to students on the first day of class is ... this is as good a place as any to think about the problems presented by counterinsurgencies and nation-building, because much of what we talk about happens right here on the Missouri-Kansas border.

"So often the Federal commanders were facing the same problems: trying to figure out which of these people were friends, who was neutral and how you had to win those people over, how what worked in one village one day may not work in the same village the next."

Both Rafuse and Beckenbaugh emphasize that their views expressed for this article do not reflect any official policy or position of the military history department, the U.S. Army or its Command and General Staff College, or the Defense Department or federal government.

The decisions to be made by the boots-on-the-ground officers rotating through Fort Leavenworth are often guided by a new doctrine developed at the fort just a few years ago — Field Manual 3-24, Counterinsurgency.

Linked most closely with the new doctrine was Gen. David Petraeus, who commanded the fort at that time. Later sent to Iraq to lead the successful troop "surge," he put in motion many new directives.

Afghanistan was his next and greater challenge, and the doctrine's effectiveness there is still an open question. Meanwhile, the general is returning to take charge of the Central Intelligence Agency.

Rafuse: "The problems Petraeus addressed would have been very familiar to Gen. Thomas Ewing when he was here on the Missouri-Kansas border."

Ewing emptied much of four Missouri border counties of residents, loyal or not, to dry up support for the guerrillas.

It hardly won many "hearts and minds," but then Ewing had no manual.

The actions of Union troopers, especially those from Kansas, often created more enemies in Missouri than they destroyed. This conundrum is a major factor in how we conduct operations today among civilians in Afghanistan.

Any patrols out of U.S. outposts like Kandahar face the same challenge as when 2nd Colorado troops rode out on scouts — what they called patrols back then — and risked deadly ambushes.

"When they go in convoy from Bagram to Kandahar, the guerrillas always have the initiative, and the counter-insurgents have to react," Beckenbaugh said.

"That dynamic hasn't changed from biblical times."

And when the bullets stop flying, life can just get more complicated.

"One problem is that a neutral population helps the insurgents," he said. "The average person wants to be left alone.

"But just imagine you are on a farm in western Missouri when a group of men comes to your house dressed in Federal uniforms. You feed them and give them what they want. And you don't want to be saying things like 'I hope you track down those bushwhackers' because what if these men are guerrillas?

"So the civilians were terrorized into a neutrality in Missouri. That is kind of what the Taliban are doing, only they are not wearing American uniforms."

## PERSONAL DEMONS

The troopers from Leavenworth were familiar with the Wornall House on what was then the road to Fort Scott. As commander of the 7th Kansas Cavalry, the original jayhawkers, Col. Charles "Doc" Jennison briefly used it as a headquarters early in the war.

The Wornall family living there was terrified, believing John Wornall, a slaveholder, could be taken out and shot at any time. Only when the feared Jennison good-naturedly traded knives with Frank, the little boy of the house, did the family relax.

During the 1864 Battle of Westport, Jennison was back, leading a different regiment, the 15th Kansan, charging south on the road. Another of Frank Wornall's memories was the amputated limbs tossed out a window of his home, used as a field hospital.

The war resulted in perhaps 50,000 amputations and launched a prosthetics industry. In 1866, one-fifth of Mississippi's state budget went to artificial limbs for its veterans.

While the experts then worked with cast iron, rubber and whittled barrel staves, a new revolution in artificial limbs for today's wounded features microprocessors, exotic metals and silicone.

A more defining aspect of the current wars are those who return home burdened with personal demons often called post-traumatic stress disorder.

The first evidence that some Civil War veterans suffered this condition as well was contained in the 1997 book "Shook Over Hell" by historian Eric Dean, who examined the case records of 291 Civil War veterans at the Indiana Hospital for the Insane.

The symptoms are familiar: depression, anxiety, "flashbacks," alcoholism, addiction and suicides. The names for it were more romantic then: "nostalgia" or "soldier's heart." Later it was summed up as "shell shock" or "combat fatigue."

Roger Spiller, a Leavenworth military historian who has written about PTSD, notes that the first professional literature describing the condition did not appear until around the turn of the 20th century.

"There is no question in my mind about it," Spiller

## CULTURAL ECHOES OF THE CIVIL WAR

America's great struggle 150 years ago changed our culture and customs, from the churches we attend to the cash we put in the plate. Some ways in which the conflict has stayed with us:

### WAR CORRESPONDENTS

The war turned news coverage into something familiar now — a feeding frenzy.

Thanks to the telegraph, the reporters' accounts of a battle could be read by soldiers while they fought it, a development that then must have felt like the instant satellite transmissions of today.

The usual tone of war articles, florid and opinionated, more closely resembled modern blogging than just-the-facts writing. Journalists in the battlefield came under heavy fire, some were captured and imprisoned. One embedded with Union troops died in a massacre at Baxter's Springs, Kan..

The byline was born — the result of U.S. Army demands that newsmen in the field sign their dispatches, called "letters."

Intended to keep reporters honest, bylines also allowed some to gain fame.

Civil War photographers, private and military, captured the human toll in raw detail. Thousands of images snapped by Mathew Brady and others forever erased notions of romantic war — although Brady moved bodies for better effect.

For decades thereafter, the military censored pictures of dead U.S. troops, restrictions that eased by the 1960s.

As TV footage flickered nightly from the combat fields of Vietnam, American opinion turned against the conflict.

In the Iraq war, the Bush administration for years banned the photographing of returning coffins.

### RELIGION

Slavery split three of our largest denominations — Baptists, Methodists and Presbyterians — in lasting ways.

The Southern Baptist Convention was formed in 1845 after Northern Baptists objected to a slaveholder being named a missionary. A similar controversy drove Southern bishops to break from the Methodist Episcopal Church and form the MEC (South), which begat the Southern Methodist Church.

Presbyterians divided into a variety of "schools," with a Deep South faction known during the Civil War as the "Presbyterian Church in the Confederate States of America."

In Kansas City, Second Presbyterian Church was formed as an anti-slavery congregation — and it remains a thriving church, now located near the Brookside area. Other local churches splintered, but reunited after the war. Some offshoots of the national denominations eventually did the same, but ideological divisions persisted.

The Southern Baptists have grown to become our largest Protestant denomination.

### CULT OF JESSE JAMES

In film, books and song, Missouri's bushwhackers keep popping up.

None has the pop-up power of Clay County's Jesse James. Maybe the worst injustice dealt the ex-Confederate guerrilla, dead for almost 130 years, was being cheated out of a fortune in royalties.

Icons of culture seem divided on how to portray James: Bruce Springsteen in a 2006 recording chose the folk-hero version ("Jesse was a man, a friend to the poor/ He'd never rob a mother or a child"). That was a year before Brad Pitt depicted him as a borderline psychotic murdered at the hands of Bob Ford.

To Southerners, the postwar robberies by Jesse and Frank James were fair retaliation, Robin Hood-like, against Northern interests.

But villainy reigns in the bulk of the Hollywood fare, which is voluminous. One online site tallies no fewer than 59 films and documentaries dating to 1908's "The James Boys of Missouri."

Reels of celluloid have been committed, as well, to the Missouri-Kansas border strife. While Clint Eastwood played an avenging south Missourian whose family fell victim to Kansas Red Legs in "The Outlaw Josey Wales," most of these movies sympathize with the brutalized residents of Lawrence.

The 1999 film "Ride with the Devil" rightly portrayed the invading guerrillas as baby-faced and longhaired. Leader William C. Quantrill was only 26, after all.

A 1940 feature, "Dark Command," cast 42-year-old Walter Pidgeon as Will Cantrell, modeled after Quantrill. In this depiction, John Wayne's marshal rewrites history by saving the town from the raiders.

World War II hero Audie Murphy starred in two films about the guerrillas; in one, 1950's "Kansas Raiders," he played a young man wrongly set to hang for helping torch Lawrence: You got it. Jesse James.

---

said. "All wars have produced casualties like this, but it just didn't fit into our frame of references."

The suffering hardly fit into the frame of reference of the mid-19th century, either.

"The United States embarked on a new relationship with death," wrote Drew Gilpin Faust in her book "This Republic of Suffering: Death and the American Civil War."

Before, people almost always passed away at home, with gathered loved ones to observe the last breath, wash the body and perform the comforting ceremonies. It did not often occur at a hospital, which were largely for the indigent, much less on a field paved with the bodies of comrades.

Both North and South had expected a quick war; what they got shocked nearly everyone, except William Tecumseh Sherman, who was running a streetcar company in St. Louis when the war broke out. His reaction to Lincoln's first call for 75,000 soldiers to rally to the Union flag?

"Why, you might as well attempt to put out the flames of a burning house with a squirt-gun."

Our house divided burned for four long years; Maj. Gen. Sherman did his part in adding to the flames — and the casualty lists, starting with the stunning numbers of dead at Shiloh.

It got worse: Three days at Gettysburg killed more than 6,000.

For context, U.S. forces, fighting for 10 years, have lost just slightly less in Afghanistan and Iraq.

Neither Washington nor Richmond had a system for publishing casualty lists, much less performing the notification functions that American military families take for granted today. Newspaper reporters did much of the collecting of names of the dead and wounded.

## HOLIDAYS

Credit black South Carolinians for introducing a ritual now called Memorial Day.

On May 1, 1865, thousands of African-Americans just freed from slavery gathered at a former Confederate prison in Charleston to honor the graves of Union men who died there.

According to historian David Blight, the occasion marked the first "Decoration Day," a holiday soon made official in state laws across the nation (if, for many years, on different dates).

Also recast: Thanksgiving.

Until 1863, states set their own dates for feasting and counting blessings. Lincoln established a fixed date — the last Thursday in November. He asked Americans not only to give thanks but to "fervently implore the interposition of the Almighty Hand" to bring peace.

## BASEBALL

Originally "townball," America's pastime in its early forms was a highbrow diversion before war broke out. Baseball owes its mass appeal, however, to troops who played it on both sides of the divide.

Batters were "strikers," runs were "aces," errors, "muffs."

Little evidence exists that Union Gen. Abner Doubleday wrote the modern rules. Most likely, the game evolved through countless contests within and between regiments.

Sometimes soldiers ran the bases while enemy troops enjoyed the game from the cheap seats of the next hill.

A year after the war, local veterans formed a club, the Antelopes, that played on a field near McGee and 14th streets.

## HABEAS CORPUS

At the time, it was an unprecedented move by a U.S. president. But in suspending the right of arrested people to file for legal recourse from their jail cells, Lincoln didn't exactly start a trend.

Until the war on terror, arguments over what the Constitution calls "the privilege of the writ of habeas corpus" were rare. And they should have been, since government is constitutionally forbidden from suspending prisoners' rights "unless when in cases of rebellion or invasion the public safety may require it."

Yet Lincoln did it..."with the deepest regret," he said. Citizens thought to be disloyal were imprisoned — thousands across Missouri — and brought before military commissions. Congress voted its approval.

(Settle down, Dixie sympathizers; Jefferson Davis suspended habeas corpus, too.)

Lincoln rationalized that the South committed the most egregious of acts, taking up arms against the government. In the Union's defense, he asked, "are all the laws, but one, to go unexecuted, and the government itself go to pieces, lest that one be violated?"

A year after Lincoln's death, the Supreme Court came to a different decision. It ruled the government can't try Americans before military tribunals so long as civilian courts are functioning.

Fast-forward 14 decades and the high court considered it again: Could the Bush administration deny U.S. citizen Yaser Hamdi — deemed an enemy combatant at the center of an alleged "dirty bomb" plot — the right to challenge the reasons for his imprisonment?

The justices delivered the same answer as in 1866: No.

## OUR MONEY

Suppressing the Southern rebellion meant soldiers, weapons, rations, horses and ships — in other words, lots of money that Washington did not have.

Lincoln's Treasury chief, Salmon Portland Chase, first created small demonination bonds and notes, some repayable on demand, to allow small investors, such as families and small shopkeepers to show their support for the war.

These "demand notes" became a kind of a national currency in 1861, a step toward the Federal $1 "greenbacks" — not backed by gold — introduced the next year. Those bore the likeness of Chase, who hoped to supplant Lincoln in the White House in 1864. Before then, paper currency had been printed by private banks, with more than 10,000 different kinds in circulation.

Also, to raise money, Lincoln in 1862 signed a bill creating the first Federal income tax — 3 percent on incomes between $600 and $10,000 and 5 percent on higher earners. The cigarette tax, too, debuted.

---

Dog tags were not issued, although one could buy metal IDs. Soldiers kept identifying letters or Bibles in their pockets; before battles, some grimly pinned scraps of paper bearing their names to their tunics.

After the fighting at Byram's Ford on October 23, 1864, Sgt. George Combs wrote home that he had held back from following his unit south so he could keep the body of his dead brother, James, an officer in the 7th Missouri State Militia, out of a mass grave.

"I had him brought to this place (Kansas City?) and put in a metallick coffin and nicely buried. When times gets a little better I will have him brought home."

So many disappeared nameless into trenches that spiritualism had a heyday as parents and wives tried to contact loved ones "on the other side."

"The Civil War soldier's biggest fear is that they would not be remembered," said Lee Ward of Independence, who maintains his own Museum of Funeral History in his home.

One Southern officer dying in a Kansas City church after the Battle of Westport left a twisted paper containing a lock of his hair.

"Take it, ma'am," he implored Elizabeth Millet, a volunteer nurse. "Someday someone will come asking for George Lucas. It will be my wife. You can give her that."

Visitors to Ward's museum quickly realize that it's not only the 150th anniversary of the Civil War.

It's also the 150th anniversary of embalming in America, a practice that had been little seen outside of medical schools before. Chemically preserving corpses for shipment over long distances and a last viewing before burial won wide acceptance.

Ward: "People have to have some way to remember,

# FOLIO OF LOCAL FEDERALS

This display of Union fighters was made possible thanks to the National Park Service, Collection of Wilson's Creek (WCNB); State Historical Society of Missouri, Columbia (SHSM); Kansas Historical Society (KHS); Missouri Valley Room, Kansas City Library (MVR); Lone Jack Civil War Battlefield Museum (LJBM) and the Kansas Heritage Center, Dodge City (KHC); Nebraska Historical Society (NHS); and the Rick Mach Historical Archives Collection (RMHAC).

**◄ Capt. Henry Palmer**
This A Company, 11th Kansas Cavalry officer often patroled out of Westport, where he found a bride. His company was in almost continuous fighting from Oct. 20-23. He recounted being caught with his pants off at the Battle of the Little Blue and fighting in his drawers. (NHS)

**◄ Capt. William A. Long**
The Company A commander, 2nd Battalion, Missouri State Militia, posed with his brother, James (right). Long died of his wounds four days after the battle of Lone Jack. (LJBM)

**▲ Capt. William Blair**
Officer of the 4th Missouri State Militia, killed Oct. 23, 1864, trying to lead Company B across the Blue River at Byram's Ford. (WCNB)

**◄ David Wood**
Son of Lt. Col. Samuel N. Wood of Sixth Missouri State Militia. Enlisted as a musician, he served as orderly and was given a fancy uniform (note the officer's shoulder straps). (WCNB)

**◄ 7th Missouri State Militia troopers**
These tough, bushwhacker-fighting units were prone to execute civilian men found to be giving the guerrillas food or information. Unique to Missouri, these regiments were paid for by the federal government but served only in this state. (LJBM)

**▲Three 15th Kansas cavalrymen**
(unidentified) posed in a Weston street. (RMHAC)

and embalming contributes to that. It is through viewing that we remember. We have to tangibly see that person, and I speak from 50 years of experience."

Thomas Holmes of Brooklyn — considered the father of modern embalming — went to Washington and embalmed bodies for free, exhibiting his work in storefronts in Georgetown and Alexandria.

Faust noted the unprecedented and massive Federal program between 1865 and 1871 that found and reburied 300,000 soldiers — Union only. This effort led to 74 more national cemeteries, beyond the five established at battlefields during the war, as well as hard feelings among white Southerners, who then conducted their own private reburials.

## 'NOBODY IS SAFE'

One of the smaller national cemeteries is in Jefferson City. A stone marker there notes the names of dozens of men who died — many with their hands up in surrender — at a little rail stop called Centralia.

Their remains had been buried beside the tracks, then later relocated more than 50 miles south to a resting place deemed more suitable.

The stone is part of the reason that Beckenbaugh thinks, "A majority of books written on the Civil War are almost uniformly on the eastern theater.

"Americans have this romantic idea of Johnny Reb and Billy Yank. But out here it is a lot nastier, a lot meaner. That makes a lot of people uncomfortable."

At Fort Leonard Wood, a senior leaders class has

**▲ Pvt. John Berry**
Fighting with Company H, 8th Missouri State Militia, he left the Lone Jack fight with a broken right shoulder, probably from a clubbing. (LJBM)

**Col. "Doc" Jennison ▶**
Even in hunting garb, he terrorized Missourians before, during and after his tenure leading the 7th Kansas Cavalry, the original "Jayhawkers." At the Battle of Westport, he led the 15th Kansas Cavalry, but lost it for his treatment of Missourians. (WCNB)

**Sen. James Lane ▶**
This militant pose may be from the spring of 1861, when he and other armed Kansans barracked in the White House until a regular troops arrived to protect the U.S. capital. He restored sagging political fortunes at the Battle of Westport and was sent back to the Senate in early 1865, but shot himself in 1866. (WCNB)

**Pvt. Curtis Casey, Pvt. Dwight Chappell, Pvt. Edgar Cone, Sgt. George Ferris ▶**
Their 7th Kansas Cavalry created more rebels than it killed along the Missouri border so Union commanders sent it to Tennessee. (KHS)

**▼ Lt. Col. George Hoyt (center) with officers of the 15th Kansas**
Hoyt had served on John Brown's defense team before the war, then became an officer in the 7th Kansas. He preferred being chief of the infamous Red Legs, however, before joining the 15th. Several officers in this regiment ended up court-martialed, but Hoyt was elected Kansas attorney general after the war. (KHS)

**◀ Maj. Henry Curtis**
Son of Maj. Gen. Samuel Curtis and adjutant to Maj. Gen. James Blunt, chief of the District of the Frontier. He was moving south with Blunt's escort when it was hit by William Quantrill's guerrillas. Run down, Curtis surrendered his pistol, only to be shot with it. (WCNB)

looked back at the Civil War. David Chuber, historian at the U.S. Army Chemical School, recalled leading non-commissioned officers to the Wilson's Creek battlefield near Springfield in 2005.

Interesting, the future platoon leaders said, but this was a conventional battle, not what they were dealing with then in Iraq. U.S. forces had become an occupying army propping up a fragile government in Baghdad and recoiling from sudden, demoralizing insurgent attacks.

So Chuber took the sergeants to Centralia, a hamlet where guerrillas stopped a train and massacred two dozen unarmed Union soldiers on furlough. Then, when a Federal force pursued them, the guerrillas pretty much wiped them out, too.

The students found the Centralia of 1864 instructive.

"We talked about ambush and psychological operations," said Chuber, "about how the guerrillas came into town on a mission not only to find intelligence but also to intimidate. Stopping that train was like controlling a main road in Iraq or Afghanistan. Troop morale will be affected if supplies can't go up and down.

"Also, if about 150 guys died in what seemed a matter of minutes, then it seems like these guerrillas can do anything, and nobody is safe."

While the conflicts of today are vastly more complex, plenty of hard-to-miss similarities cast shadows from the old war that haunt forces today.

"I don't need to connect the dots for my students," Beckenbaugh said. "They do it themselves."

# Grim legacy of massacres still haunts the region

By **RICK MONTGOMERY** ★ THE KANSAS CITY STAR

Other places in the country had Civil War battles. Missouri and Kansas had massacres.

No word better fits the September 1864 attack by guerrillas riding onto a field of Federals near Centralia, Mo.

The mounted charge "became a scene of murder and outrage at which the heart sickens," reported a Union officer. "Most of them (U.S. soldiers) were beaten over the head, seventeen of them were scalped...

"One man had his nose cut off. One hundred and fifty dead bodies have been found."

A year earlier, Lawrence buried nearly 200 people after William C. Quantrill and his raiders plundered the town.

But such guerrilla atrocities were not the only bloodletting in the region.

Federal officers were quick to assemble firing squads in Missouri. And a massacre of Southern prisoners most likely occurred after the 1864 Mine Creek battle.

"The war in western Missouri and Kansas is more brutal and barbaric than anywhere else," said Ar-

Missouri and Kansas saw more than their share of massacres and innocent people killed on an almost weekly basis. Southern sympathizers, whether guerrillas or supporters or sometimes innocent but unlucky men faced Federal firing squads throughout the war. | LESLIE'S ILLUSTRATED

nold Schofield, superintendent of the Mine Creek Battlefield State Historic Site. "You have Union Missourians capturing Confederate Missourians at Mine Creek. And they don't like each other. They hate each other..."

Between them and the Kansans, who cared little for Missourians since the bloody 1850s, "it's all about retribution, retaliation, revenge," he said. "The war

# CIVIL WAR MASSACRES

THE KANSAS CITY STAR

out here is just..."

A pause, a sigh: "...different."

In the first months of the war, Kansans commanded by U.S. Sen. James Lane incinerated Osceola, Mo., and had perhaps a dozen men shot.

This was well before Union leaders elsewhere warmed to the tactics of "total war," destroying the property and homes of civilian populations.

"They learned the art of total war out here," said Schofield. But even "total war" in the East rarely passed

muster for a "massacre."

"Massacres are a touchy subject," Missouri State University historian William Piston noted. "The losing side often uses the term where a victor might not."

The leading indicator is a lopsided casualty count, often with more dead — many from head shots — than wounded or taken prisoner.

Piston said just a half dozen needless deaths, people murdered rather than held captive, could qualify as a massacre. That applies to any number of incidents here, including:

## OCT. 18, 1862

Before a crowd of spectators in Palmyra, Mo., a firing squad shot 10 Confederate prisoners sitting at the foot of their open coffins.

The execution was ordered when a missing Union informer, already dead, was not returned as demanded. The Union officers picked out their victims from a pool of uninvolved prisoners. While the action was criticized, even in the London Times, the officer in charge soon made general.

## MAY 18, 1863

From a report by Maj. Tom Livingston, a feared guerrilla leader of southwest Missouri:

"On the 18th, my scouts reported 60 negroes and white men, belonging to Colonel Williams' negro (the 1st Kansas Colored Infantry) regiment, with five

six-mule teams, foraging on Centre Creek Prairie. I ordered out 67 of my best mounted men ... routed them, and pursued them about 8 miles. ... The enemy's loss in killed was, negroes, 23, and 7 white men. ... I sustained no loss."

Black soldiers who fell into the hands of Confederates often were slaughtered, such as at Fort Pillow in Tennessee or Poison Springs in Arkansas.

## AUG. 21, 1863

George Gaston Elliott, staying at the Eldridge Hotel in Lawrence, recalled the day: "One glance was enough to reveal the character of the catastrophe. ... Dead bodies could be seen along the sidewalks. ... Any attempt to escape only provokes a fatal shot from a revolver."

Only one of Quantrill's raiders died amid the slaughter, a man so drunk he was not aware when his comrades left. At least three others were too wounded to ride; they were found in a buggy near the state line and quickly finished off by furious Kansans.

In the coming days, Kansans tried to even the score. Sen. Lane, who barely escaped into a Lawrence cornfield, howled for the chance to wipe out Westport and Independence in return:

"I want to see every foot of ground in Jackson, Cass and Bates counties burned over. ... Missourians are wolves, snakes, devils, and damn their souls, I want to see them cast into a burning hell!'

Abraham Lincoln did not agree. Still, his army commanders scoured Jackson and Cass counties. Any man found wearing a new coat was likely to be shot down on suspicion of having stolen it from Lawrence.

Then Gen. Thomas Ewing ordered that western Missourians across four counties leave their rural homes. As they were packing to leave farms near Lone Jack, a half dozen Missourians, age 17 to 75, were marched off and shot by Kansas troopers.

## OCT. 6, 1863

With Jackson County too hot for comfort, Quantrill led his band to Texas to winter. On the trip, he managed to wipe out nearly 100 soldiers at Baxter Springs, Kan.

A few men were fatally caught outside little Fort Blair's walls, but most who died were in an approaching and unsuspecting Union column escorting Maj. Gen. James Blunt. Many of the bushwhackers wore stolen blue uniforms, confusing the Federals who quickly broke and ran. The rebels chased down victims, taking no prisoners, including the musicians in Blunt's band. A 12-year-old drummer boy was gunned down with the rest. One survivor had five gunshot wounds to his face, which, an army surgeon said, "could not be recognized as belonging to a human being."

## SEPT. 27, 1864

The Centralia massacre featured two parts, almost equally appalling.

In the morning, mayhem visited the railside hamlet in the form of William "Bloody Bill" Anderson. His bunch was drinking and robbing when the whistle of a North Missouri Railroad locomotive was heard from the east.

The captured cars carried about two dozen unarmed Union soldiers on furlough. The bushwhackers removed them from the train, stripped them and shot all but one. (Sgt. Tom Goodman, kept for a prisoner exchange, would escape and write a book.)

Centralia, part two, unfolded south of town. Companies of the 39th Missouri Infantry, largely green recruits wielding single-shot muskets and mounted on farm horses, rode in, viewed the bodies and went looking for revenge.

They entered a trap. Confronted by only a fraction of their foes — many more were hidden in the brush on both flanks — the Federals dismounted for a long-range exchange of fire. They got off only one volley before being overrun. Many surrendered, yet it did not save them. The horse holders were chased back to Centralia, where another Federal company was largely wiped out.

The guerrillas suffered two or three killed, while about 120 Union troops lay dead, many still in the rank in which they had stood. So closely arrayed were they that guerrilla Dave Pool decided to walk on them, not touching ground.

## OCT. 10, 1864

In present-day Concordia, Mo., bushwhackers led by Pool and George Todd mowed down about 45 of the "damned Dutch," as the German immigrant farmers were called.

Staunchly loyal and anti-slavery, but poorly trained, the Germans set up an ambush near a place called Cook's Store. They were promptly routed.

"What occurred afterward reminded me of a rabbit hunt in the country," recalled John McCorkle, who later wrote of his years with Quantrill. "The boys started in the brush and every few minutes out would run a Dutchman and the boys on the outside would start after him. Not one of them escaped."

Other German militiamen were chased into a cornfield, and "very few of this company reached home alive," McCorkle said.

## OCT. 25, 1864

Maj. Gen. Sterling Price's army was in retreat from the Battle of Westport and bottlenecked at the Mine Creek crossing just inside Kansas when two Federal cavalry brigades caught up with it.

"It was like rolling thunder," said Mine Creek's Schofield. The Union troopers "go right through the Confederate line like a hot knife through butter."

Confusion spread in the blinding black-powder smoke, in part because many poorly equipped Confederates wore blue, having snatched Union overcoats and jackets to ward off the chill.

About 300 rebels died. The Union force, though outnumbered almost 3 to 1, reported only eight dead. Some today argue it was merely a rout, not a massacre.

But records and recollections make it clear Union officers ordered many captives, mostly those in blue garb, to be shot.

A newspaperman, either naive or complicit, offered another clue.

"One remarkable fact is worthy of mention," he wrote smugly. "Nine of every ten rebels killed or wounded are shot in the head — showing the accuracy of the aim of our boys."

Men firing pistols from galloping horses usually are not so accurate.

# The hinge of fate swung favorably for Kansas City

The infant City of Kansas was a horrible place when hostilities erupted.

And horribly lucky when the bloodshed ended.

Armed and violent, muddy, mocked by traveling writers, deeply cleaved in its landscape and politics, our town managed to hang on and then soar. Soon after the Civil War, Southerners and Yankees here were whooping it up over securing the first railroad span across the Missouri River.

Imagine if the war had gone differently.

If it rages a few years longer or starts a decade earlier, if the Confederacy somehow prevails, I think Kansas City dies on the vine.

No bridge means no sprawling stockyards, no big packing houses. It probably means, a century later, no skyscrapers, no Truman Sports Complex.

The city on this bend of the Missouri was just get-

**AUTHOR'S ESSAY**
Star reporter Rick Montgomery co-wrote "Kansas City: An American Story," a historical and pictorial narrative of the city from birth to the present day.

ting started, incorporated in 1850, when violence marred Kansas' quest for statehood. Steamboats carrying Kansas-bound abolitionists from the East often unloaded at the rock landing near today's City Market.

More than 25,000 emigrants and visitors filled our shabby hotels between 1856 and 1858 to venture in and out of "Bleeding" Kansas. The town's population ticked up toward 5,000.

Ohioan Robert Van Horn came in 1855 and soon ran the leading newspaper. In one eye-rolling example of turning every minus into a plus, his paper offered regrets that the border parties "have concluded to go to war and settle their difficulties by bloodshed, but … we wish to remind them that they can buy powder and lead of (local) merchants at St. Louis prices, and other military supplies much cheaper."

Van Horn and other boosters saw railroads as the ticket to prosperity. But the war dried up venture capital. Tracks laid on the levee only went a few miles east. The Missouri Pacific, creeping west through guerrilla country, had only reached Sedalia. A fledging Kansas Pacific tied Kaw valley to Lawrence. Going anywhere north meant booking a steamboat.

Someone eventually would leap the untamed Missouri — but where?

On the river's Kansas side, Leavenworth boasted 3,000 more people, was safer due to its protective fort and flourished from the war trade.

Upstart Kansas City, for all its bluster, was knocked as a slave-owning gully town, ridiculously carved into bluffs and peppered by rude Southerners.

A Cincinnati reporter visited KC and found: "The people here all seem partly demented in regard to their prospects."

Nobody was said to sleep without a pistol under the pillow. "Red shirts, bowie knives and pistols openly worn on the girdle were everywhere seen," Theodore Case wrote.

A "malignant stronghold of persecution and violence," wrote New York Tribune editor Horace Greeley, who passed through in 1859. He, like many, envisioned Leavenworth as America's next great city.

During the war, perhaps a third of Kansas City's residents hightailed it. Nearly all businesses changed hands, failed or were shuttered by Union soldiers. Even Westport founder and Southern sympathizer John Calvin McCoy relocated temporarily to Glasgow, Mo.

Count among U.S. loyalists Van Horn and town builder Kersey Coates. But few saw Abraham Lincoln's election as a good thing; he mustered one vote out of every 19 cast across Jackson County.

Like all Missouri towns, ours stayed in the hands of those in blue uniforms, but bushwhackers and Red Legs made a trip of a few miles into the countryside perilous. Mail coaches from Independence to Kansas City often were interrupted.

Coates' young daughter, Laura, growing up near Fort Union, recalled "a bullet whizzing through our bedroom window" and a rebel spy dangling from a scaffold near Wyandotte and 13th streets.

By 1865, a Federal officer reported Jackson County so depleted, he could not raise another full company of militia — 100 men.

All of which makes the postwar success so stunning.

Not only did dueling sides make peace, they locked arms to make money — with a jackpot of iron spanning the river.

Businessmen of Southern persuasion Charles E. Kearney and lawyer John W. Reid teamed with Van Horn and Coates to romance the Hannibal & St. Joseph Railroad. The locals let railroad executive James Joy line his own pockets by handing him land in the scrubby West Bottoms — sure to soar in value with a bridge.

By 1866, Van Horn, now a Republican congressman, snuck though a bill providing federal authorization of a Kansas City bridge, catching Leavenworth and Atchison rivals flatfooted.

It came to be called the Hannibal Bridge, opening in 1869. Our July Fourth party that year drew national attention. With the Transcontinental Railroad's Golden Spike just hammered in Utah, the media hyped anything train-related.

The bridge linked the Southwest's cattle to Chicago and the hungry East beyond. Having won what one called "the race for importance," Kansas City's population zoomed from roughly 3,500 in 1865 to 32,000 in 1870.

I wonder again: Would any of it have occurred had the Civil War played out differently?

Suppose the South wins and, in a brokered peace, acquires slave state Missouri? That keeps Van Horn out of Congress in 1866. Missouri's future would be tied to a Dixie economy more dependent on river travel and exports than on inland rail freight.

As it happened, Kansas Citians entered peacetime pining for a break — with bridge plans in hand and investors ready to gamble. "War's end turned everyone's attention to the West, a project of national importance," said Peter Hansen, a former Kansas Citian who edits Railroad History magazine.

How ironic: One of the shakiest points on the map when fighting began, the City of Kansas found itself in the perfect spot.

# Kansas City 1864

The 1860 census, taken before the whirlwind hit Kansas City, tallied 4,418 residents and at least two dozen saloons (not counting Lucy's ice cream and oyster saloon on Main Street). Like the rest of Missouri, the town was sharply divided between loyalists and secessionists, but it would be held by Union forces throughout the conflict.

By **DARRYL LEVINGS & DAVE EAMES**

★

The KANSAS CITY STAR

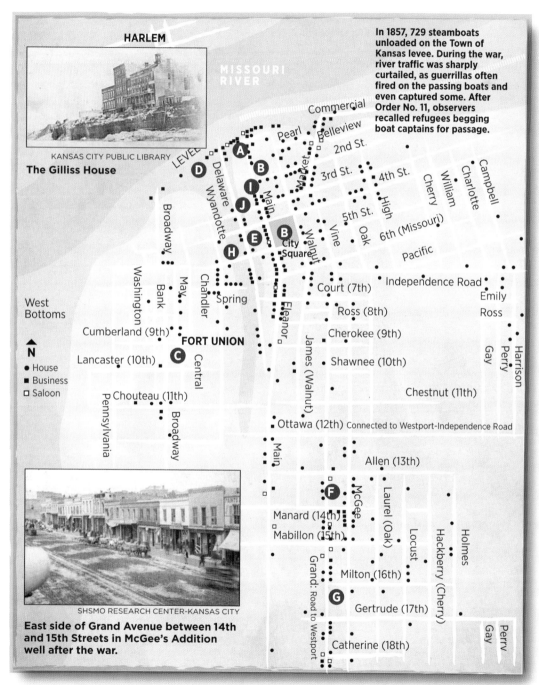

**HARLEM**

KANSAS CITY PUBLIC LIBRARY
**The Gilliss House**

In 1857, 729 steamboats unloaded on the Town of Kansas levee. During the war, river traffic was sharply curtailed, as guerrillas often fired on the passing boats and even captured some. After Order No. 11, observers recalled refugees begging boat captains for passage.

West Bottoms

N
● House
■ Business
□ Saloon

**FORT UNION**

SHSMO RESEARCH CENTER-KANSAS CITY
**East side of Grand Avenue between 14th and 15th Streets in McGee's Addition well after the war.**

**A** **THE WESTERN JOURNAL OF COMMERCE**, the most influential newspaper, was owned by one of the most influential men, Robert Van Horn. Running for mayor, Van Horn narrowly defeated a secessionist candidate at a crucial time. Union men were ridiculed or pummeled on the streets, but Van Horn was handicapped — the police commissioners leaned Southern. He went to St. Louis to confer with powerful Republicans and secure some Federal troops from Leavenworth to keep the peace.

**B** The Union flag flapped over the **PUBLIC SQUARE**, but secessionists raised their own at Second and Main streets, visible from the river. When Leaven-worth troops landed, Van Horn would remark with satisfaction: "In an hour, not a flag save Old Glory was visible anywhere."

**C** Soon, **FORT UNION** was occupied by Van Horn's Battalion of Volunteer Reserve. It was organized with American, German and Irish companies, the latter captained by the artist George C. Bingham. The old howitzer at the gate of the earthwork fort signaled emergencies. One girl recalled: "The cannon was constantly repeating the signals of alarm given by the pickets stationed on the outskirts of the city; the heat of every inhabitant quickened by the sound. Indiscriminate shooting continued among the guards..." The fort's stables were across 10th Street in the board over basement of what was to be Kersey Coates' big hotel.

**D** **THE GILLISS HOUSE**, a hostel on the levee, was at times known as Claiborne House, the Western, the

**Fort Union** | COURTESY KANSAS CITY PUBLIC LIBRARY

American and the Eldridge. Owned at one point by the anti-slavery Emigrant Aid Society, it hid Territorial Gov. Andrew Reeder during the Kansas troubles. When a rebel army threatened in the fall of 1864, Maj. Gen. Samuel Curtis used it as Union headquarters.

**E** **PACIFIC HOUSE** was HQ for Gen. Thomas Ewing, chief of the District of the Border, who was holding the bag when William Quantrill raided Lawrence in 1863. He issued Order No. 11 to neutralize the border by largely emptying four Missouri counties.

**F** **THE THOMAS BUILDING** in McGee's Addition was used to imprison Southern women on its second floor. When the Cockrell Building, used as a guard-

house, collapsed next door in August 1863, it brought down the jail. Five women died, outraging guerrillas, who were next seen in Lawrence's streets.

**G** The Union hospital operating in Milt **MCGEE'S HOTEL**, also known as the Farmers, Southern, or Planters, probably was where the injured women were taken. It was chosen probably for having been a Southern meeting place. It was part of McGee's Addition that straddled Grand Avenue, upon which Santa Fe-bound freight went to Westport.

**H** **THE METHODIST CHURCH, SOUTH,** was used as a hospital for wounded rebels after the 1864 Battle of Westport. Edward Scarritt, 11, was there with his

Kansas City grew from a waterfront town — as in this view from 1871 — into a thriving metropolis.
But its success depended on many factors relating to the Civil War. | SHSMO RESEARCH CENTER KANSAS CITY

mother who pitched in as a nurse. "Some of the soldiers were mortally wounded and were sending dying messages through the dear women to their loved ones at home," he recalled. "Some were bitterly bemoaning their fate and all were hushed into stillness when it was announced that a comrade had closed his eyes to earthly scenes and was 'slipping o'er the brink.'"

**❶** One of the many **MAIN STREET GROG SHOPS** got customers it didn't want one night in 1862. Coleman "Bud" Younger wrote how he, George Todd and other bushwhackers slipped into town for a bit of killing. At the bar, Younger recalled, "I called for a cigar, and glancing around, saw that we had been recognized by a trooper who had been playing cards. He reached for his pistol, but he never pulled it. I do not know how many men were killed that night..."

The bushwackers escaped east on the road to Independence.

**❿** **"A BRICK HOUSE OF ILL REPUTE,"** reported the Journal, burned on a March evening in 1862. "We didn't hear any body cry fire, consequently, we came to the conclusion that nobody objected." Another such house "occupied by several women light of love" was east off the Independence road. "Drinking was deep and the orgies shameful," wrote a bushwhacker — until they blasted the soldiers through the windows — without hitting any of the soiled doves. A last detail of Yankee depravity: "Piled two deep the dead men lay, one with a glass grasped tightly in his stiffened fingers, and one in his shut hand the picture of a woman scantily clad."

George Todd's guerrillas gunning down Union soldiers in the saloon, from John Edwards' "Noted Guerrillas, or the Warfare of the Border."

SOURCES: 1860 CENSUS, CITY MAPS FROM 1860 AND 1878.

# PVT. DANIEL ROUTT'S LAST LETTER HOME:

# 'YOU WILL HAVE IT TO REMEMBER ME BY'

*Pvt. Daniel J. Routt of Company C of the 7th Missouri State Militia sent a letter with a lock of his hair to his wife, Chinece, back home with two children under 3. He refers to the first Battle of Independence on Aug. 11, 1862, when secessionist forces made a successful dawn attack. Days later, Routt's unit left Lexington to look for the rebels. At Lone Jack, a southeast Jackson County hamlet, they found a hornet's nest of surrounding Confederate recruiting camps. In the vicious five-hour battle on Aug. 16, Routt was killed.*

Dear wife This Day is one great excitement in Camp wee received a disptch yestereday Evening from independence calling on Col Huston for reinforcements for that place Stating that our men that are stationed were there attacted By an overwhelming force of rebels the reinforcment was sent but alas it was to late the rebels being 1500 strong while our men Numbered less than 400 after 3 hours of Desperate fighting had to Surrender our boys that went to relave only about 200 men got in a few miles of thir and heairing that the fight was over hured back to this place wee are looking every hour to bee attacted by them at this place but wee have been reinforced and think that wee will be able to whip them. our cllonel sais he is Determined not to Surrender that he will Burn the place first wee are all well and feell like fighting.

Wee hope that these lines may find you all well enclsed you will find the lock of hair that you requested and in case that never see me again you will have to it to remember me by as long as you live I sent you ten dollars som days ago but have not yet an answer from it yet since that time have sent you my picture... i will now come to a close Dear By requesting you sufer no uneasiness about me if we have a fight and I do not get killed I will write to you imediately and let you know the particulars of it you will Remember me in your prays Tell Tempy that her pa is glad that She has not forgotten him tell luther that his pa sais that he must be a good boy and that his pa loves him and thinks about continually Dear this request i have to make and then i am done you must be sure to raise the children up right raise them to be truthful and have them to be obedient to you and you will have not truble with them

You loveing husband

COURTESY OF LONE JACK BATTLEFIELD AND MUSEUM

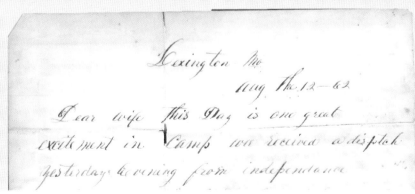

# History stays alive in memory of woman

By **BRIAN BURNES** ★ THE KANSAS CITY STAR

**GENERATIONS**
**A series of family memories about local ancestors in the Civil War.**

Most Americans today do not have the personal, physical link to the Civil War soldier that Martha Noland has.

She sat in the lap of one.

Her recollection is dim. After all, she was only 2.

"I remember that he was redheaded, with a reddish beard and a very sandy complexion," Noland, now 88, says of her grandfather. "I remember his heavy high-topped black shoes, I guess because I was low to the ground."

She had accompanied her parents on a Sunday visit to Foster, Mo., the Bates County village where the elderly John S. Millsap lived.

She did not understand until decades later that upon reaching the age of 16, her grandfather had enlisted in the 9th Missouri State Military Cavalry, a regiment created to find and fight the deadly bushwhackers swarming the state.

The 9th Missouri Cavalry dueled with "Bloody" Bill Anderson, George Todd, John Thrailkill and others. They got to Centralia on Sept. 28, 1864, the

Martha Noland holds an enlargement of a tintype photograph of grandfather John S. Millsap as a Union private. Noland has a dim recollection of seeing him in the 1920s and has spent more than 40 years finding out more about him. | TODD FEEBACK, THE KANSAS CITY STAR

day after guerrillas massacred two groups of Union soldiers. The officers ordered the innocent townspeople to gather and bury many of the 140 bodies.

A detachment of the 9th also took part in the Battle of Westport. Under the command of Gen. John McNeil, it splashed across the Little Blue River and pushed Maj. Gen. Sterling Price's Confederates through Independence.

But Noland, who now lives in Kansas City, North, was unaware of all this until after 1967. "After my mother died," Noland says, "every time I found something out about her father, I thought: 'What a shame.'"

Shame?

Like of lot of family matters, it's complicated.

Two years after the war, John Millsap married Nancy Isabell Hallam and reared nine children on a Platte County farm just west of Interstate 29. The eighth, born in 1890, was Bessie, Noland's mother.

Around 1900, John and Nancy divorced. Five years later, he took a second wife. Like most of the Millsap children, Bessie was distressed by the split, refusing to discuss it in any detail.

"Perhaps she was worried the divorce would be considered a stigma," Noland says. "In those days, you didn't talk about private matters, and you were a little concerned about what other people might think. I think she was embarrassed by it.

"But life went on in those days and you didn't contemplate the past. She was a busy farmwife, cooking and tanning and raising her own children."

Still, to Noland, it's a shame her mother couldn't share in what's been learned.

"She would have been very interested in knowing

*If the picture is a wedding portrait, Millsap quickly has grown balding and whiskered, seemingly much aged from the teenager who, just a few years before, had brandished his revolver before the camera for a period tintype.*

these things."

Among Noland's findings:

A 1913 application for a federal pension showed Millsap mustered out in July 1865 at Benton Barracks, just north of St. Louis. The 66-year-old veteran eventually would receive a $50 monthly amount.

Company muster rolls that record Millsap's occasional extra payments, such as in June and October 1864, when he accepted 25 cents for putting in service a personal gun sling, or in December 1864, when he received 36 cents for a ball screw and screwdriver.

Records revealing his death on Jan. 24, 1925, at age 77 and noting that his second wife later collected the $30 widow's pension. Millsap is buried in St. Matthew's Cemetery in Riverside.

Histories noting how the regiment lost 108 men: 31 killed and mortally wounded, the remaining 77 taken by disease.

No eureka moments, but Noland keeps digging.

What she has recovered amounts to a three-ring binder thick with microfilmed documents, photocopies of handwritten recollections and fragile newsprint under plastic.

Among the handful of family photos today held by Noland is a portrait of John and Nancy, who married in 1867. If the picture is a wedding portrait, Millsap quickly has grown balding and whiskered, seemingly much aged from the teenager who, just a few years before, had brandished his revolver before the camera for a period tintype.

The tintype was given to her just a year ago by a relative, who weeks later died of pneumonia.

"Obviously, I was very fortunate to get that tintype,"

Noland says.

Noland has found no wartime writings or journals of Millsap. Her only samples of his handwriting are the faint pencil script on two postcards he mailed to Noland's mother not long before his death in Fort Scott, Kan.

"My dear Bessie this leaves us all in pretty bad shape ... they were going to take me to Fort Scott hospital ... I am getting worse all the time ... is the best we can do ... so be good kiss my babies goodbye ..."

During her years of research, Noland has tracked down distant cousins across Missouri, but many of the details she seeks seem lost to time.

Today Noland is a board member in the Platte County Historical and Genealogical Society and assembled the Civil War exhibit now on display at the Ben Ferrel Museum in Platte City.

It's important to keep curious. She has two grandsons in their 20s "not that interested right now," Noland says. "But it's still worth it, passing on that information."

And that tintype.

What does Noland think of when she looks at it?

"That he was a very strong Republican who loved his country."

John S. Millsap and his wife, Nancy Millsap, pose after the war. Their marriage, which produced Martha Noland's mother and eight siblings, broke up in 1890.

# BY THE NUMBERS

## CONFEDERATE FORCES: 1,082,119

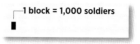

Before the Civil War, the nation had lost only about 15,000 men in its conflicts. Imagine, then, the shock more than a half million dead in a space of four years. No other war since has matched its carnage. The Federal armies, larger, lost more men in total than those of the South. But, proportionally, the rebel soldiers suffered higher mortality. The records of the Confederacy are more fragmentary that the Union lists of casualties.

**Unscathed veterans: 590,093**

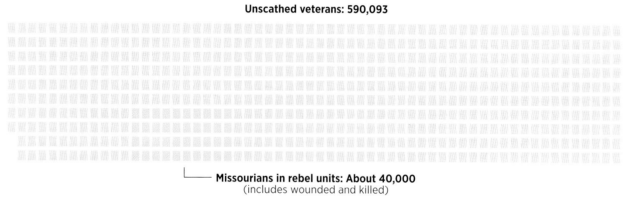

**Missourians in rebel units: About 40,000**
(includes wounded and killed)

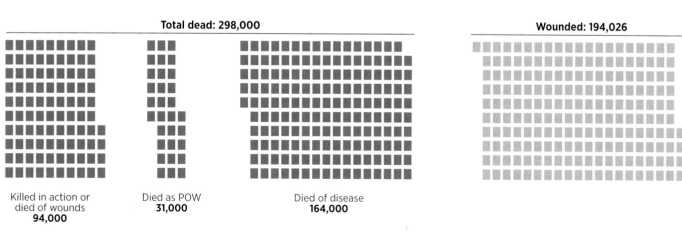

**Total dead: 298,000**

Killed in action or
died of wounds
**94,000**

Died as POW
**31,000**

Died of disease
**164,000**

**Wounded: 194,026**

# BY THE NUMBERS
## UNION FORCES: 1,556,678

1 block = 1,000 soldiers

**Unscathed veterans: 275,175**

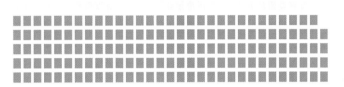

**Black soldiers: 154,346**
(includes wounded but does not include killed)

**Missourians in Union units: 96,662**
(includes wounded but
does not include killed)

**Kansans in Union units: 17,467**
(includes wounded but
does not include killed)

8,300 black Missourians; number of black Kansans, estimated 2,500

**Wounded: 275,175**

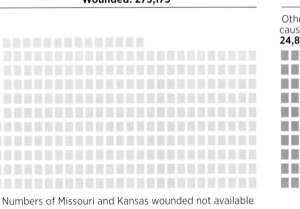

Numbers of Missouri and Kansas wounded not available

**Total dead: 389,753**

| Other causes 24,881 | Died of disease 224,580 | Died as POW 30,192 | Killed in action or died of wounds 110,070 |
|---|---|---|---|

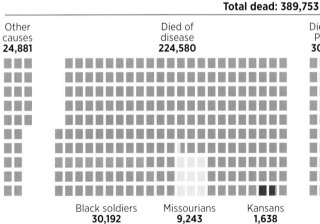

Black soldiers **30,192**  Missourians **9,243**  Kansans **1,638**

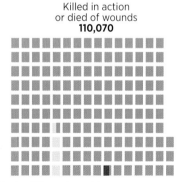

Black soldiers **2,751**  Missourians **3,317**  Kansans **737**

# SOME THINGS YOU MAY NOT KNOW ABOUT THE WAR BETWEEN THE STATES

By **DARRYL LEVINGS** ★ THE KANSAS CITY STAR

The Civil War provides a seemingly inexhaustible supply of facts and stories. Amaze your friends, confound your know-it-all brother-in-law with these little-known nuggets of our history. Did you know that...

**The nation's first monument erected to honor Union war dead may be in Woodlawn Cemetery in Independence.**

It was dedicated July 31, 1864, to troopers of the locally stationed 2nd Colorado Cavalry, killed in skirmishes and ambushes by local guerrillas. Poet Ellen Williams, a camp follower and wife of a bugler in the regiment, composed the words that today are nearly erased by weather:

*"Brave heroes rest beneath this sculptured stone*
*In unfair contest slain by murderous hands.*
*They knew no yielding to a cruel foe —*
*And thus, this tribute to their memory stands*
*Our country's honor, and a nation's pride*
*'Twas thus they nobly lived and bravely died."*

This was done well before the monument to

Monument to fallen members of the 2nd Colorado Cavalry, erected in 1864 in Independence.

Union dead dedicated at Manassas, Va., (Bull Run) in June 1865. Southerners, however, likely put up the first monument of all, also at Manassas. There, a crowd of 1,000 gathered Sept. 4, 1861, to dedicate a memorial to fallen Col. Francis Bartow, a Georgian famous for his last words: "My God, boys, they have got me, but never give up the field." That marble obelisk disappeared the next year, but another marker replaced it around the turn of the century, when most Civil War monuments were raised and dedicated.

**The first black regiment recruited in Missouri was called the 3rd Arkansas Infantry.**

The subterfuge was to avoid offending or frightening whites in Missouri. Later, the unit would be designated the 56th U.S. Colored Troops.

**A Kansan had the honor of being the first soldier to be executed in the Civil War.**

In an argument, Pvt. Joseph W. Cole of the 1st Kansas Volunteer Infantry Regiment pulled a knife and stabbed another soldier to death. Cole was executed by Gen. Nathaniel Lyon's command on July 14, 1861, in Greene County, Mo. By the end of the Civil War, a total of 267 Union soldiers would be executed.

## The CSS Missouri was the last Confederate ironclad to surrender.

This sounds brave and defiant until one realizes the boat had been constructed far up the Red River in Shreveport, La., and could not descend the shallow river. The Yankees never got far enough upstream during the war to confront it.

**USS St. Louis** | COURTESY OF U.S. NAVAL ARCHIVES

## One Union soldier fighting at the Battle of Westport would later become the title character in a movie, played by Robert Redford.

Second Colorado Cavalry Pvt. John Johnson was probably born John Garrison. In the movie, he is "Jeremiah Johnson," but on the frontier, he sup-

posedly was "Liver-Eating Johnson," for the tale that he devoured the livers of his Indian enemies.

## Union Cemetery in Kansas City holds the grave of a Civil War Medal of Honor winner, who had enlisted the day before his heroic action.

Nathaniel Gwynne, 15, earned his medal the hard way, losing an arm and taking two bullets in the leg while charging across a Petersburg, Va., battlefield to recapture some Union colors from Confederates. Ending up a Kansas City lawyer and real estate agent, he served as a representative in the Missouri House, where he sponsored veterans' benefits legislation. He died at age 33.

## The USS St. Louis was the first U.S. ironclad gunboat.

Launched Oct.12, 1861, at Carondelet, Mo., it was the first of James Eads' ironclads to sustain a bombardment from a hostile battery, leading the Federal fleet in victories at Island No.10 on the Mississippi and at Fort Henry on the Tennessee.

## The statue of Shakespeare in New York's Central Park was erected with the help of John Wilkes Booth, who had trod the boards in Leavenworth less than a year earlier.

Booth starred in several Shakespearean favorites with a traveling troupe and was in St. Louis in early 1863 when he was arrested and fined for wishing "the president and whole damned government would go to hell!" On Christmas Eve of that year, the Leavenworth Daily Times remarked that Booth had played the Prince of Denmark at the Union the night

**Booth**

before. "Hamlet had a cold — and so did the audience." Joining brothers Edwin and Junius in November 1864 to raise funds for the statue, he played Mark Antony in "Julius Caesar" — a single performance billed as "the greatest theatrical event in New York history." At the time, he was plotting to kidnap President Abraham Lincoln. Five months later, he shot him at Ford's Theatre in Washington.

**The last slave in Missouri may not have gotten her freedom until 24 years after the war.**

The 1889 death of a central Missouri farmer, Joseph Hickam, resulted in an unusual probate case in Boonville. A black woman named Eda, who had worked in his home, alleged she was never told that slavery had been abolished back when she was a 16-year-old girl. She filed suit for $1,400 against his estate for lost wages at $5 a

month. A judge decided to split the difference at $785, but the family appealed. Four Hickam v. Hickam civil trials later, in which no one could prove whether the woman had been deceived, jurors denied Eda any back pay.

**A Union officer at Westport would end up saving the presidency of Andrew Johnson.**

Maj. Edmund Ross of the 11th Kansas Cavalry was appointed to the Senate seat vacated by James Lane's suicide. As the Radical Republicans tried to push Johnson out of the White House, Ross became the deciding vote in the trial. Originally counted as a safe aye for impeachment, Ross soon displayed a disturbing sense of fairness. He faced tremendous pressure, including a telegram that read: "Kansas has heard the evidence and demands the conviction of the president. Signed D.R. Anthony (a Leavenworth newspaper publisher) and 1,000 others." Once his "not guilty" vote saved Johnson, Ross was ruined politically. Just how his fellow Kansans felt about him was illustrated by a message from the chief justice of the Kansas Supreme Court suggesting: "...the rope with which Judas Iscariot hanged himself is lost, but Jim Lane's pistol is at your service."

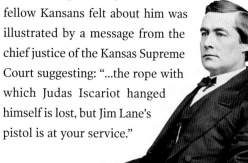

## THE STAR'S CIVIL WAR QUIZ

**1** Reuben "Rooster" Cogburn, the fictional hero of two "True Grit" movies, rode with Quantrill at Lawrence. Where did he lose his eye (it changed from the left to the right between films)?

**2** Gen. John S. Marmaduke got fellow Confederate Gen. Lucius M. Walker to spit out his insufferable toothpick. How?

**3** Something is wrong with the gravestone of guerrilla chief George Todd in Woodlawn Cemetery in Independence. What is it?

**4** Which town was the first to be served by a railroad in the 1860s: Kansas City, Weston or Wyandott City (Kansas City, Kan.)?

**5** What street in Kansas City is named for a fallen Civil War soldier?

**6** A Missourian captained a gun crew in the great ironclad duel between the USS Monitor and the CSS Virginia (known to some as the Merrimack). Who was it?

**7** Of the 500 or so correspondents and artists who covered the Civil War, only one appears to have been killed in action. Who was it and in what part of the border area did he meet his end?

**First bonus question:** A Civil War cannon called the Parrott can be seen in the southern part of Loose Park in Kansas City. Both sides manufactured this type of gun, and there is little difference between them. What side would have made this particular gun, and how can you tell?

**Second bonus question:** A Missouri West Point graduate was at the First Battle of Bull Run as a Union officer, then switched sides and became a Confederate officer. Who was it?

**Answers on Page 154**

Part 5

# Forward march

The war's lessons will have relevance for generations to come,
but are we doing enough to keep them alive?

By LEE HILL KAVANAUGH & RICK MONTGOMERY ★ THE KANSAS CITY STAR

The Civil War is over. Everyone who lived it, dead as dinosaurs.

But seemingly on every weekend, somewhere in the United States, the blue and gray rise up again. Thousands step into 19th century shoes to "feel" the history.

Sara Pelis, mother of eight, grandmother to four, was packing for her entire family before a re-enactment event at Wilson's Creek near Springfield, where they would join 3,000 others like them.

All traveling back in time.

For weeks, Pelis sifted through her fam-

As Union troops fired, a re-enactor in their midst took shots of his own during the Aug. 14, 2011, restaging of the 1861 Civil War Battle of Wilson's Creek south of Springfield. | ALLISON LONG, THE KANSAS CITY STAR

-ily's stash of historically authentic clothes, camping gear and cooking ware like the quartermaster of a small army. Her family tries to be accurate when they re-enact, turning away from the modern world as much as they can.

The 43-year-old Pelis leans in close for confession: They still "farb out," the term scornful, hard-core enthusiasts use for those re-enactors who sneak in a cellphone, sip pop from a can or pull out a disposable wipe.

Her family's most egregious sin behind the flaps of a sultry, buggy tent? "Fans from Walmart," Sara whispers. "Battery operated."

The Wilson's Creek sesquicentennial, earlier this month, was a vivid reminder of how far we've moved on. Such observances will continue until 2015. But after they end, who'll spin this history forward?

Could the Civil War and the power of its lessons fade like so many sepia photos?

Given the horrors of that war — particularly where Missouri meets Kansas and wounds haven't wholly healed — some may argue for writing off the past, or at least softening it for our politically correct classrooms.

Scholars maintain that history itself can help heal. Filmmaker Ken Burns, who in 1990 produced a Civil War documentary that sent PBS ratings rocketing, has cited the "medicinal" power of confronting and understanding our American narrative.

But 50 years from now, at the 200th anniversary of the conflict, will area enthusiasts still be dressing the part? Will lands be preserved, new histories written?

Will groups be discussing William Quantrill or

James Lane or Sterling Price?

"Interest is going to slide downward," says Lane Smith, president of the Kansas City Civil War Round Table, which kicked off in 1958 with Harry Truman as its first speaker.

"When this period of the 150th ends, I think there will not be the excitement until the 175th. And a lot of us aren't going to make it to then."

★ ★ ★

Along Wilson's Creek, some pre-teen spectators seemed a little bored, or scared, as horses charged and cannons boomed. Some, one suspects, would prefer to be at home with their video consoles.

John M. Sutton is chief park ranger at the national battlefield. "I've got two teenage kids and they're just into other things," he says. The youngsters he sees at the park are usually brought by parents, "then you won't see them again until they're married and have kids of their own."

The troops on the battlefield happily swallow the drifting gun smoke. But most are paunchier, grayer — their heads, not their Confederate jackets — than what history tells us of those who enlisted in the 1860s to set the course for America's future.

**The Pelis family, who took part in the Wilson's Creek re-enactment, in contemporary clothing (facing page) and their Civil War garb. James Pelis (second from left) and his wife, Sara Pelis, are surrounded by (from left) Bill, 14, Isaiah, 7, David, 10, Haley Johannes, 19 and Victoria, 12.**

| RICH SUGG AND ALLISON LONG, THE KANSAS CITY STAR

The blue and the gray met again as re-enactors march and counter-march before thousands of spectators at the re-creation of the 1861 Battle of Wilson's Creek near Springfield. | ALLISON LONG, THE KANSAS CITY STAR

At the Civil War roundtables in Kansas City, where well-read history buffs hear lectures and discuss aspects of the conflict, the demographic is even older. And overwhelmingly white — not a hopeful sign, in an increasingly diverse culture, for 21st-century recruitment efforts.

For all who dabble in learning about the Civil War, no matter the setting, a certain moment happens. A moment when they either wade deep into the genre or turn away as bystanders.

For many, the lure comes from pride of lineage traced to an ancestor who served; a history that whispers. Others stumble upon a book or story that captures their imagination.

Or it might be as simple as making a joyful noise, as a Liberty man noted while gazing at a selection of muskets:

"Black powder is like taking drugs. Once you start shooting it up, you can't stop."

Still, whole swaths of the population keep their distance. The past is the past, after all.

The loss of more than 600,000 countrymen, the shame of slavery, the grittiness of that era — when TV and toilet paper didn't exist and women hid their knees, ankles and minds — can make for uneasy conversation.

As for now, the history is mostly framed by those who try to teach it, preserve it in museums, write books or make films, argue about it and, like Sara Pelis, immerse themselves physically in it.

"Oh, kids, can one of you grab my hoop bag?" she yells upstairs.

For her part, she's preparing to wear for days this tiered contraption of concentric wooden hoops and ropes engineered to balloon a skirt or dress.

She counts the long dresses draped over a door. Another hanger holds stiff-boned corsets, cotton chemises, an array of petticoats, bonnets, straw hats. Then she holds up a billowy white item that looks … unfinished?

"Crotchless drawers," she says and laughs. Historically accurate. "People in the 1860s weren't stupid."

Maybe ours is the ignorant era: A 2009 survey of U.S. 17-year-olds found 57 percent unable to cite the half century (1850-1900) in which the Civil War and Reconstruction happened.

Public-school pupils in Missouri study state history in the fourth grade. They are "expected," but not required, to "explain Missouri's role in the Civil War as a border state," according to teaching standards.

The 150th anniversary, says Bill Gerling, a state education official, is a great opportunity to acquaint kids with regional history.

"A lot depends on the teacher."

Too much, probably.

Who has time to lather on the local history in the elementary grades when the National Assessment of Educational Progress — all-important in fixing district funding — stresses math and language?

"We'd like to go into the schools," says Smith of the Civil War Round Table, "but we don't get any encouragement from educators."

During her three years at Grandview Middle School, Courtney Cook tried to bring the Missouri-Kansas conflict to life — but only stirred up conflict with others.

Cook introduced her pupils to Confederate and Union re-enactors and encouraged the kids to try on the woolly uniforms. Sometimes she came in period garb, which some of her peers thought "distracting."

The Grain Valley woman says administrators told her to stick to a curriculum on which the students would be tested.

Cook lost her teaching job to budget reductions last year.

"You've got to teach the good and the bad about U.S. history," she says, "… and the textbooks barely list a battle west of the Mississippi."

One high school text used in local schools devotes 29 colorful pages to the war but just one paragraph to "Bleeding Kansas." (And it neglects the righteous savagery of John Brown when he was passing through.)

Cook continued: "The students have heard about Shawnee Mission Kia on TV commercials. They know Westport is a drinking place," but few know how Shawnee Mission or Westport played into the war. "They need to have that history put into their hands and take ownership of it."

It's all around us, at the Shawnee Indian Mission, where Kansas' territorial legislators debated slavery; Loose Park, site of the Battle of West-port; the Wornall House, where wounded soldiers lay.

"It absolutely makes a difference when a young person can stand at a place where history happened," says Olathe educator Maureen Donegan. She noted that parents, and not just teachers, should bring kids there.

In May, Danni Hammontree stood in an open field off Nashua Road in Liberty, stomping a shovel. Nearby, her eighth-grade classmates gazed at remnants just unearthed and placed on a plastic tarp: Inkwell caps. A bottle of Castoria oil. Horseshoes.

Liberty Junior High School teacher Art Smith finds a new place each spring, combing Clay County archives and pleading with property owners to let the kids in to dig.

Apple orchards used to grow out of this year's field. Houses 160 years old grace its edges.

"Mr. Smith does a good job not making us, but allowing us, to go back to that period," says Danni. Picking where to plant her shovel is intuitive: Where might items fall out of pockets or saddlebags? Near that creek bed where guerrillas may have bathed? On a property line — could a soldier have scaled a fence long removed?

"If you just get kids thinking about that stuff," says Smith, "half your battle is won."

★ ★ ★

Union drummer John Allin crumpled and fell as the fighting turned nasty.

So young, too. Just turned 15.

He represents the future for those who would keep at least some part of the war fresh.

But the bitter politics, then and now, turn him off. For many contemporary Confederates, President Abraham Lincoln's war led to Big Government 2011.

So when a few grown-up rebels at Wilson's Creek started swearing (modern obscenities, not just the "Lincoln lover" jabs) and hurling horse manure at retreating Federals, John just played dead by his drum.

"For some, it's all about battles. I disagree. I like the camaraderie," he later says.

After the skirmish, he marched to a stage to play percussion bones with the Short Leaf Band. In the rebel camp, rivalries dissolved as the Unionist teen plucked "Old Dan Tucker" on his banjo.

In his three years of rallying youngsters into Cass County's Civil War society, his interests have been fixed on the music of the 1860s and discovery of how kids lived then.

John founded the Civil War Kids Club in sixth grade at Cass Midway School. Now with 20 members, the club meets at the Harrisonville public library to talk history and plan outings.

The club started when John asked friends to help him make a video they called "Fire on the Border," about the Union's incendiary Order No. 11: "I invited three girls and three boys. Well, those girls eventually fell out of the club. But we've since picked up, oh, about seven others."

In the fall, they aim to raised funds for their project by taking old-time photos at festivals.

"You want to keep Civil War history alive for our youth? You use the arts," says Carol Bohl, Cass County Historical Society director. Music and theater, painting murals or stitching suspender buttons on trousers.

Leave the politics to adults.

"The question becomes, how do you prevent what festered back then ... from taking over our mindset to the point it did?" Bohl asks. "To hear the political rhetoric today scares me to death. It shows when you moralize an issue, you can't compromise on anything."

★ ★ ★

A statue of a proud Maj. Gen. Sterling Price was recently refurbished in his hometown of Keytesville, Mo., about an hour's drive from Kansas City.

A museum is dedicated to him as well, but it's a little more humble. It has no air conditioning or heat, and volunteers unlock the doors just a few days a week.

"I get people in here all the time who stop in and say their last name is Price, or they know they're related to him," says Janet Weaver. "Most of the time I have to gently tell them the war is over. And we lost."

A hearty laugh. "Museum humor," she adds.

Small-town curators and county historical societies look forward to anniversaries that draw new visitors. But often the public interest dies when the party's over. It happened after the bicentennial of the Lewis and Clark voyage, says Terry Davis at the American Association for State and Local History.

"You had these little museums pop up. But once the anniversary was done, the tourism was done," Davis says.

The Price museum, however, has been around since the Civil War centennial, and Davis is bullish on such places. "If they're engrained in their communities, I think they'll be there to stay," she says. "These small museums can do awesome work on a shoestring."

Weaver, 65, is a retired high school history teacher. She connects artifacts to old murderers and forlorn

**Liberty Junior High students, including Mikayla Gascich (left), 14, dug for artifacts at the site of a former plantation in Liberty.** | KEITH MYERS, THE KANSAS CITY STAR

Joe Hursey, 43, a military man who loves order, took over an operation resembling an antique store on steroids.

A museum needs to grab people within minutes, he says, "or else they won't come back."

He purged much of the memorabilia, reorganized some more and uncovered lost gems. Space was made for historians and anthropologists to conduct research.

The most noticeable change? The 50 enlarged portraits of Paola residents, some famous, some infamous, hung in chronological order, with placards telling their robust tales.

The museum held its first winetasting: "A night with Quantrill." And it has a traveling history show with touchable items for an audience, whether it's a nursing home or an elementary school.

Hursey's next goal: enticing the young into "owning" the museum. A Halloween festival with historical characters and games for kids is coming up.

"I'm not afraid to fail with an idea," he says. "We want to be the best history museum around these parts ... to survive and be here for the 200th anniversary."

★ ★ ★

lovers, with tales that unfold with a deep breath and "Well, the story goes..."

That rough-hewn oxen yoke hanging on the wall? "We got it, powder beetles and all," she says with pride. "It was the Price family's." Virginians, who came here when the governor/ general was a boy.

She loves questions, all but one: "Who's going to take over when you kick the bucket?" her husband often asks her. She shrugs.

"I hate the answer."

Paola, Kan., may have its own answer in the new director of the Miami County Historical Museum.

As children overwork their thumbs on the latest gadgets, historians are encouraged that technology may provide the rope to pull the Civil War into the imaginations of generations to come.

The Internet already has revolutionized the painstaking hobby of genealogical research. Tracking ancestry into the 1800s can take minutes rather than months.

Need info about a battlefield? There's an app for that.

The Civil War Trust, working with the National Park Service and a government grant, has rolled out iPhone applications specific to four battlegrounds — Gettysburg, Fredericksburg, Chancellorsville and Manassas.

Stand at any spot, punch the "Battle App" and hear experts tell what occurred beneath your feet.

"Virtual tours you can follow using your GPS," says the trust's Jim Campi. "We're using technology to reach out to a younger audience. Our hope is to do more with the western theater soon."

On the field near Wilson's Creek, the soldiers in Union uniform looked authentic. Except one was lugging, instead of a Springfield rifle, a Viper Filmstream movie camera.

His name: Shane Seley, founder of Kansas City-based Wide Awake Films. Crouched behind some timber, he tried to stay low and blend in.

But there was no mistaking what Seley, 42, was doing out there, recording the battle of Bloody Hill in high definition.

"I love these guys," he says of the troops, who high-five after combat. "It's like experiencing the positives of war without all of the negatives."

Technology's march has made every annal of history — including our corner of the Civil War — easier to call up, tune in or click. Wide Awake Films boasts the world's largest archive of stock footage re-creating Civil War action, and the explosion of niche TV chan-

**Shane Seley of Liberty, a partner with Wide Awake Films, had the vintage look as he shot footage amid the re-enactment of the Battle of Wilson's Creek.** | ALLISON LONG, THE KANSAS CITY STAR

nels, History and Discovery and National Geographic specials, stokes the demand.

A native Kansan, Seley knew little about the border conflict until he took up broadcast journalism at the University of Kansas. His interest soared as he pondered the visuals, "scalpings, saber attacks, carving obscenities on peoples' chests...," he rattles off.

Throw in video wizardry and some local actors and a Wide Awake DVD brings the brutality to living rooms, if you want it, in the award-winning "Bad Blood."

Anyone hooked on the war in the Kansas City region can drive to dozens of historical society offices and peruse the letters of soldiers or the emancipation papers of slaves.

High tech is about to make the driving unnecessary.

Researchers were looking forward to the ease of finding documents from 30 contributing organizations in a digital Civil War archive being built at the Kansas City Public Library.

The library received a six-figure grant that will help finance digitalization of unique mid-19th-century diary entries, maps and photographs from around the region. Ultimately, the library will showcase those items through an online archive, currently called "The Missouri-Kansas Conflict: Civil War On the Western Border, 1854-1865."

A planning grant last year financed a survey of the documents at archives — 25,000 pages were identified as prime for the project. Now their scanning has finally begun.

Organizers envision a tricked-up website where readers will be able to click up timelines and tools "showing them the spiderweb of connections that these historical persons, places and events have with one another," says Eli Paul of the library's Missouri Valley Special Collections.

Maybe by the Appomattox anniversary in 2015, he jokes. Until then, the digitalized documents will be parked at www.sos.mo.gov/mdh.

"I can't tell you how many times I've seen people who come to that sort of magical moment in life when one starts looking back in time as much as forward," Paul says. "And when they do, we'll be here — all the institutions contributing to the website — when they start reaching back."

Places where fallen warriors rest are more likely to strive to keep their memories alive.

So it's not surprising that northern California will be less interested than North Carolina.

Or that in Kansas, Lawrence celebrates a week of events surrounding its 1863 destruction by Missouri guerrillas.

In Nebraska, the folks of a different Lawrence prefer their annual "Cow Chip Open" at the local golf club.

"My sense is that the interest and the passions are very much alive from Washington, D.C., through the South," says New Mexico State University historian Dwight Pitcaithley.

"But in Boston, where the American Revolution is huge? I worked there 10 years for the National Park Service, and the Civil War was just not on the radar screen."

As the United States changes demographically, enthusiasm for all things Civil War may well diminish.

Newly arrived Hispanics or Asians have no cultural connection. Even the black community, which was in the middle of the great conflict, is hard to interest.

"Part of the problem is we've cast it as a white man's war," says Hari Jones, curator of the African American Civil War Memorial and Museum in Washington. "We've broken it down to these two competing, grossly inaccurate sides: The myth of the noble North bringing glory to the poor Negro. And the myth of Southerners who cared for and were liked by their slaves."

Jones says he hopes this century sheds light on a more complicated truth: Of brave and often highly educated blacks lobbying Congress, and loading their own muskets, to free themselves. Of sacrifices made by citizens of all ethnic blends in the ongoing pursuit of a more perfect union.

Knowing the details is one thing, taking away the right lessons quite another.

"We've remembered the Civil War in different ways," says James Grossman at the American Historical Association. "And remembering that it was about slavery — one of our greatest sins — is crucial.

"When a nation commits a sin so egregious, it pays a big price. That's Lesson Number 1."

"I am concerned," says Retired Army Brig. Gen. Donald Scott of Kansas City, a descendant of northeast Missouri slaves, "that the Civil War observance will give a four-year spotlight on those who will re-fight the battles and argue the causes rather than provide an opportunity for Americans to learn from our heritage."

It's a heritage blueprinted in the Declaration of Independence, a past that requires us to define who we have been, and will be, as a nation, says Scott: "Every generation faces those moments," be it women's suffrage or gay rights or 9/11.

Each compels America to reflect on the worst of moments, when a war prompted Lincoln to ask at Gettysburg "whether that nation ... can long endure."

It has so far.

Back at Wilson's Creek, temperatures climb to the high 90s. Spectators have largely fled.

**Re-enactors at Wilson's Creek Battlefield, Springfield, Mo.** | ALLISON LONG, THE KANSAS CITY STAR

Still, women wearing ankle-length dresses sit in the shade, fanning themselves. Men sip liquids from tin cups, reclining on the ground; some snooze with hats over their faces.

At the Pelis tent, a pot of stew bubbles over a wood fire. But the campsite is empty. The kids and their parents are doing what families have done for all time — cooling off in the creek, a stream of history.

"Ooooh, this is so amazing," Sara says, wading in and throwing her head back in relief.

"We've been here for five days. We camped in pouring rains and searing heat. And you know what? I could do this another five days.

"People don't know how relaxing this is. No phone calls. No computers. No Facebook! No television."

The family already is planning their next campaign:

a September re-enactment in Lexington, Mo. They've come to value what tomorrow's communities might learn, too. Remembering the war that reconnected a nation can reconnect families.

"This is something my kids will never forget," says Pelis. "I know Civil War re-enactments will go on ... because of one simple but powerful reason.

"All of this is really, really fun."

# RACING TO SAVE HALLOWED LANDS

Groups strive to keep suburban sprawl from engulfing sites where history was made.

By LEE HILL KAVANAUGH ★ THE KANSAS CITY STAR

One October day, around 7 a.m., the roaring woke Lori Wade.

Beyond a window, a bulldozer, tearing up brush, ripping out walnut trees.

No!!! STOP! she yelled, running out the door in her bare feet, still in pajamas.

STOP! This is sacred ground!

Locals have known Old Atherton Road as the place where slaves once lived and died. But with a 39-acre housing development, that history was about to be plowed under.

Wade's yelling halted the bulldozer — and put the project — into idling mode.

Mike Calvert, president of the Civil War Round Table of Western Missouri, has shared with the developer how the land once belonged to Jabez Smith. Jackson County's largest slave owner, in 1820 he'd brought perhaps 300 black families from Virginia, settling them in a tent city on the hill.

Archaeologists conducted a grid search with ground-penetrating radar. Revealed were anomalies consistent with mass graves. One of the cholera epidemics of the time?

Calvert knows how "progress" can bulldoze the past. He worries as well about land not far away on which the 1864 Battle of the Little Blue was fought. It won't be long before the Lewis and Clark Expressway gobbles up some of those acres.

Across the nation, Civil War battlefields disappear by an acre a day.

Organizations like the Civil War Trust are struggling against the pizza shops and big-box stores encroaching on the hallowed grounds where a nation struggled to define itself.

Once an often futile and scattershot fight, preservation has been helped by the 1990 creation of the Civil War Sites Advisory Commission.

Jim Lighthizer, president of the nonprofit Civil War Trust, announced in March that so far his group had saved 30,000 acres.

Encouraging every American to donate $1.50 to the Give 150 program, the trust intends to acquire, preserve and restore to a natural state 20,000 acres more before the war's sesquicentennial ends in 2015.

"One of the big reasons Civil War lands are endangered is this feeling that goes back generations: 'This land has always been farmland and always will be,' " said Jim Campi of the trust. "It's usually too late when we realize that's not the case."

He called today's sluggish economy "a two-edged sword." New development means jobs — tempting communities to write off historic property. But when recession drives down values, it presents bargains to preservationists.

About 25 miles south, Civil War enthusiasts in Lone Jack see no such a bargain.

Inside the Civil War Museum of Jackson County is a diorama of the 1862 Battle of Lone Jack, something of a dollhouse of horror. Tiny struggling soldiers with faces of angst; horses dying of wounds; and beyond the struggle a view of a bucolic field where 2,000 rebel fighters crept before their surprise attack.

Once visitors look at the diorama, museum volunteer Dan Hadley steers them to a spot just outside the museum. Looking west is the same field, the same view, now covered in soybeans.

"You can just imagine it, can't you?" he says.

"That's why this is so precious."

Of 945 acres where bullets flew, only this field is unaltered. The 30-plus acres, zoned for commercial use, is next to U.S. 50 east of Lee's Summit. Its price: more than $1 million, too much for the nonprofit Friends of Historical Lone Jack.

Still, the group has not surrendered to sprawl. It won a $55,000 federal grant for a land usage plan, the first step to buy land through more grants or gifts.

But it's a race.

"In 50 years there could be a gas station here or a strip club for that matter, and we would be an island in the middle of the suburbs," Hadley says.

He points to "progress": A neon sign advertising a Sonic fast-food restaurant, a strip mall behind it, just steps from where the fallen soldiers are buried.

"Welcome to the subchapter of battlefield preservation," sighs Hadley.

If more research on Old Atherton Road confirms human remains, the group wants to honor the site. And christen the ground with a new name.

For more than 100 years the hill was known by a name passed down from generations. A name so ugly that even historians cringe when they say it.

"There are 200 to 300 souls who we don't have a face for, and we don't have a name for. ... They lived in servitude," said Calvert.

"You may not like that history, but you need to remember it."

# A RARE PHOTO EMERGES OF KEY PLAYER IN QUANTRILL SAGA

Morgan Walker's possessions were coveted by Kansans. But Quantrill, who set up the raid, then warned the Missourian..

Even after 150 years, new historical finds bubble up and excite history enthusiasts.

Not long ago, Anne Jacobberger, who lives in the San Francisco area, was going through an old album that had come down through her mother's family.

In it was the rare, if not the only, photograph of Morgan Walker, who lived in the Blue Springs area just before the conflict.

Largely forgotten, the farmer was a key player in the saga of William Clarke Quantrill.

**Morgan Walker**

It was Walker's 30 slaves, fine horses and gold that a band of Kansas abolitionists slipped across the state line to steal in late 1860. Among them was Quantrill, who set up the little raid and then went ahead to warn Walker's family.

Three Kansans were killed as a result of the waiting Missourians' ambush, one by Walker with his Hawken rifle — a head shot on a running man. Walker was not a man to be trifled with.

Despite Quantrill's turncoat role, some of the Jackson Countians believed he needed hanging as well. It may have been then that he made up the story of how he and his brother were on their way to Colorado when waylaid by jayhawkers, and his brother, entirely fictional, was killed. He used the story for the rest of the war.

Walker's home ended up burned like so many in the county, but Jacobberger's photographs survived because of one of Walker's sons, Sidney Walker. He had emigrated to northern California.

"I do a lot of genealogy," Jacobberger said, so she puzzled out the photographs, many without identifications.

"Somebody did a drawing of Morgan Walker, and, oh yeah, you can see the resemblance."

And now she wants to donate the image and others from the album to one of the border region's universities.

"They'll be valuable to future scholars. There's always a graduate student who will come around and eventually use them.

"They're not my blood relatives," she explained. "The Civil War does not attract the interest here that it does in your part of the country. I figure the pictures should come back to Missouri. They'd be more historically significant there."

## A LETTER FROM THE BATTLE OF WESTPORT:

# 'YOU KNOW NOT THE TROUBLE I HAVE SEEN'

*Lt. James L. Combs of the 7th Missouri State Militia cavalry had survived the fierce little fight at Lone Jack, but his luck ran out two years later during the Battle of Westport. On the morning of Oct. 23, 1864, his regiment had to cross the Blue River on foot under severe Confederate fire. His brother, George, a sergeant, noted how James was hit before even reaching Byram's Ford at the river. His commander, Col. John F. Phillips, would later tell of rushing down the road and seeing the dying officer lying against a tree. The young man saluted and said, "Colonel, I am shot to death." As he recalled for a Kansas City Times reporter in 1912: "I dismounted and lifting his head on my knees I gave him a sip of peach brandy I carried and then I had to leave him there. I shall never forget his face." The grieving sergeant kept his brother from going into a mass grave, perhaps temporarily interring him in Union Cemetery, and then sent the sad news to his pregnant sister-in-law, Sarah Goff Combs of Henry County. On Oct. 28, 1864, the day George Combs wrote this letter from Kansas City, the last battle in Missouri was occurring in Newtonia. His regiment already was returning northward with rebel prisoners. Other than chasing down bushwhackers and their supporters, Sgt. Combs' war was pretty much over, too.*

**Lt. James Combs**

Dear Sister it is with great sorrow that I have to find myself in communicating to you the sad news of the Death of Poor James he was killed on Sunday the 23rd between independence and westport we were formed in line about sunrise to make a charge on the rebels and we had not advanced ten steps toward the rebels when he was shot through the bowels. I was standing by his side when he fell I picked him up and carried him back out of the lines and laid him down and he said he would like to see you again, but he new that he never would he said he was willing to die he lived until dark that evening he suffered very much through the day. I had him brought to this place and put in a metallick coffin and nicely buried When times gets a little better I will have him brought home You know not the trouble that I have seen Our men pushed on after the rebels and I was left on the Battle field among strangers and had no one to help me much about taking care of my Dear brother. I am going to start to the command to morrow which I learn are at Fort Scot They have bin fighting ever since they left independence Price is on the run There has bin a great many killed and wounded. Richard Jones is wounded in the leg You must excuse my letter, my trouble is so great that I cannot write so good."

**Springfield rifle, $675.** Black powder starts around $20 a pound; don't forget to purchase the percussion caps.

# Dressing the part

By LEE HILL KAVANAUGH ★ THE KANSAS CITY STAR

Something almost magical happens when you put on historically accurate clothing from the Civil War era, says Jean Warren at James Country Mercantile.

"It's a lot easier to forget you're in 2011."

The Liberty store, co-owned with husband Del, has been around some 25 years, selling a wide selection of historically accurate items, and books and DVDs. This is the place where the 21st century man, woman or child can walk out fully dressed for the 19th century.

The store caters to the needs of both the brand new Civil War re-enactor or the established living historian. Items range from toothbrushes to tin cups, coffee pots to petticoats, and more.

Even the store's name was inspired by the era:

James Country because of the store's proximity to the James boys' stomping grounds. But as much fun as the store has, it's also one of the world's best known in the re-enacting niche market. And Jean Warren knows as much about how people lived every day 150 years ago as anyone.

"I've shipped orders to Civil War re-enactors who live in England who are in a group called the American Civil War Society. Also to people in Norway, Denmark, Germany, France, Poland, Australia, New Zealand and even Japan," she says. "I'm not surprised anymore."

There's no question that the Civil War niche market will grow even more the next four years, she says.

"But it will change drastically after that."

Del Warren, 64, is the store's gunsmith, a craftsman who makes historically accurate guns. He's also the field seller traveling to Civil War events around the United States. At Wilson's Creek, their sutlery tent was always open well into the nighttime hours.

The future looks good for a new demographic of younger people passionate about all things Civil War, the couple says.

"It will still be thriving," says Del Warren. "Even though I won't be around for the 175th, let alone for the 200th, I know our clothes and guns will be. They're made that well."

**Kepi, $40.** Western-ers on both sides were more likely to wear slouch hats, same price.

**Smoothside Canteen, $40.** Okay, it's non-authentic stain-less steel, but if you want tin, drink rusty water; the casing is covered with either blue or gray wool, depending on which side is swilling.

**Belt and buckle, $12 to $20.** Confederates liberat-ing them from prisoners or union dead could brag by turning the buckles upside down.

**Trousers, $35 to $70** depending on size and fabric. Yankees must wear regulation; but proper "rebels" have a wider choice.

**Military jacket, $75 and up.** Many styles: Colum-bus Depot for Southern-ers shown; regulation sack coat for Yankees.

**Civilian shirt, $30.** For a fancier bush-whacker shirt, embroidered by the ladies with big pockets for cartridges, $100 and up.

**Shoes, $50 and up.** Called ironclads in the war, look for rough brogans.

**Corset, $100 and up.** Sorry, a must for a proper 1860 silhouette; has to be custom-fitted.

**White chemise, $20 to $30.** Keeps the corset from scratchin'.

**Camp dress, or bodice and skirt, $75 and up.** Hand-sewn triples the price. In Missouri, most hard-working rural women didn't wear hoops. Only for Sunday best.

**Rope Petticoat, $50 to $60.** Everything ankle-length to avoid stirring up the men folks.

**Split-crotch drawers, $20.** Breezy and not necessary; you can cheat on anything invisible.

**Footwear, $20 and up?** You can cheat here. Buy knock-off, lace-up boots. No black running shoes.

# TREASURES OF THE CIVIL WAR

By DARRYL LEVINGS ★ THE KANSAS CITY STAR

The best Civil War museum in the region is surely the Sweeny Collection now held by the National Parks Service at Wilson's Creek National Battlefield.

Closer and very good are state collections at Lexington, Topeka, Lone Jack and Mine Creek, just down the state line in Kansas.

But look around. Little treasure troves of Civil War artifacts and stories are all around us in county museums and other collections. The Star visited several and asked the curators or directors to single out just one item that they thought was unique or special to their collection. It often wasn't easy to choose.

## ST. JOSEPH MUSEUM

Sarah Elder, curator of collections, is proud of its new displays and especially fond of a **piece of cutlery used by Gen. Elijah Gates.**

Fighting from Arkansas to Atlanta, the tough rebel was captured three times and wounded five. In the vicious battle at Franklin, Tenn., both his arms were hit; Union surgeons amputated the left. It didn't stop him from escaping in about three weeks.

Later sheriff, state treasurer and U.S. marshal, Gates got along with this implement — a cutting knife with fork prongs at the end.

"Even losing an arm in battle, having this, no problem," Elder noted.

## MISSOURI STATE MUSEUM

It is not the porcelain-face doll that intrigues curator Julie Kemper, but **the toy's pretty white gown,** the "Jakey Dress," with the delicate pink print. Before her Uncle Jacob "Jake" Romans went off to a Union outfit, he delighted 4-year-old Estella Lindsey with a fancy dress.

"In 1864, a group of men came to the house, some kind of guerrilla fighters, and took what they wanted and then started to burn the Lindseys' possessions," Kemper said in the Capitol's new and revolving Civil War exhibit.

But one raider relented and retrieved from the flames the dress for the sobbing child. When Estella outgrew it, her mother made the doll's dress from the fabric.

"It was something that she could treasure through the war."

## KANSAS HISTORICAL SOCIETY

**The flag of the First Kansas Colored Infantry** is a favorite of Blair Tarr, curator of the Kansas Museum of History in west Topeka. He thinks the regiment was ignored too long.

"Out here on the frontier, black soldiers really led the way in the Civil War. Everybody credits the 54th Massachusetts (heroes in the film "Glory"), but these guys were in the service long before the 54th was even created."

## JACKSON COUNTY CIVIL WAR MUSEUM

Dan Hadley, vice president of the battlefield museum in Lone Jack, points to **an old broadside advertising the 24th battle anniversary picnic at Lone Jack**. As years went by, the once largely local and Southern event drew all from the area.

"Thousands of people showed up. It became one of the biggest events of Jackson County."

Politicians would speechify, contests would be held, ice cream freezers would be cranked.

One young attendee who had come in the family's wagon would return as a politician to give his own stump speeches from the band stand. Even later, Harry Truman advocated building the battlefield's circular, stone museum building.

## LEXINGTON HISTORICAL MUSEUM

A great many Civil War weapons found their way to a great many display cases across our land. The route of **Col. James Mulligan's sword** to this one is a little off the beaten track.

The Union officer, defeated at the siege and battle of Lexington, of his blade to Gen. Sterling Price, who graciously declined. But it was stolen and hidden by a rebel deserter.

Surfacing after a half century, it was given in 1912 to Mulligan's widow — the unlucky colonel had been killed in 1864 at Winchester, Va. After her death, said volunteer director Roger Slusher, "her daughter, who was here as a baby, sent the sword back to the town as a thank you."

That was in 1917. The recipient stuck it for safekeeping in a bank vault, where it stayed hidden for another half century and more.

## MIAMI COUNTY HISTORICAL MUSEUM

The thing that one notices first about this museum in Paola, Kan., is the photographs, old portraits blown up huge, marching in chronological order around the room. The second thing, perhaps, is the bullet hole square in the forehead of **Abraham "Bullet Hole" Ellis**. Put there by William Clarke Quantrill when Ellis looked out a window during a raid in 1862.

"Quantrill said he didn't mean to shoot him, but it was a good shot," said director/curator Joe Hursey.

Oh, well then, fine. But wasn't Ellis drilled in Aubry, in the next county? Yes, Hursey agreed, but Ellis was superintendent of schools in Miami (then Lykins) County. Before the war, he had approved Quantrill as a teacher, which is why the bushwhacker considered Ellis his friend and apologetically mopped the blood off his face.

## BATTLE OF LEXINGTON STATE HISTORIC SITE

Somebody in Waverly thought it just fine to take a shot at the Federal gunboat passing by — until the gunboat tied up and began lobbing fat cannonballs into the little town.

"A great scattering of personnel and gentlemen but little other damage" resulted. Among the "personnel" was a Cherokee who scouted for Quantrill, Squirrel Tail. His picture is above the **shell, which much resembles a bowling** ball. "It's very heavy, but was used on a newel post by a family," said resource manager Janae Fuller. "That's why it has the hole drilled in it."

JEFF DAVIS.
TAKEN FROM LIFE.

## RAY COUNTY MUSEUM

In the Civil War Room, Linda Emley first shows a Union uniform, then an unusual musket, then a flag.

But what's that in a case beneath a revolver?

**An old envelope is printed with the caricature of Jefferson Davis hanging by the neck** — after a whiskey barrel has been rolled from beneath his feet.

Mostly in the first two years of the war, both sides printed perhaps 6,000 different, collectible envelopes with patriotic sentiments. The Northern printers were not adverse to execution themes or boldly displaying "Death to Traitors" on their wares. As the reporter leaves the old Richmond house, Emley asks: "Would you like to

see the meat grinder that was at the house where Bloody Bill Anderson had his last meal?"

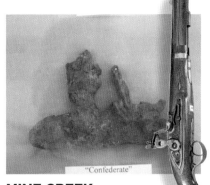

"Confederate"

## MINE CREEK BATTLEFIELD STATE HISTORICAL SITE

What Arnold Scofield likes most in the collection here is a fast-firing Spencer carbine that was actually used by a victorious Yankee on this battlefield. But it's not here right now.

So we look into a case showing all the different types of bullets dug up around the site. And the eye seizes on a chunk of corrosion that most would throw away, **an old lock plate that once held a flint**.

It was old even for the Civil War, when most handguns had graduated to revolving. There's probably a story behind it. Another ill-armed Southern recruit who decided to join up with Maj. Gen. Sterling Price in the 1864 invasion of Missouri and then found

himself in hurried retreat through this part of Kansas. What became of him?

"They grabbed a weapon off the mantle and they jumped on their favorite horse and they joined up," said Schofield, site historian and a premier Civil War authority in the region. "They were the ordnance's officer's nightmare."

## BATES COUNTY MUSEUM

The old ledger indicates that the Bates Countians were, if not God-fearing, at least a taxpaying people. Line after line, numbers and names in that beautiful script show their property and the amount to be rendered unto the county government.

These folks got ripped off.

"At least the 60 percent who didn't come back," agreed museum director Peggy Buhr.

**The ledger is from 1863** — before September — when every last farmer and merchant, woman and slave, child and dog, more than 6,000 in all, were forced to leave fields to fall fallow and property to be burned. Because Bates had no towns with a Union garrison, it suffered worse under Order No. 11 than Jackson or Cass counties.

How did the old book survive? The courthouse was burned. Who pro-

tected the book? Where was it taken? When was it returned?

Buhr: "These are all mysteries."

# Five buried in the 'Six-Man Cemetery' were his kin

By **MARÁ ROSE WILLLIAMS** ★ THE KANSAS CITY STAR

**GENERATIONS**
A series of family memories about local ancestors in the Civil War.

Not far from Lone Jack is a little enclosure with an old, white marker. It was once topped by a stone dove, later loosed by a thief.

The "Six-Man Cemetery," some call the place.

Bob Potter is kin to five of them.

"The cemetery also has been called 'The Confederate Cemetery,' " he says. "I don't know why. There are no soldiers buried there."

All civilians: two great-great-grandfathers, Benja-

min Potter and John S. Cave; two great-great-uncles, William and David Hunter; a distant 17-year-old cousin, Andrew Owsley; and neighbor William Tate. All slain Sept. 6, 1863.

"It was a big part of the family," Potter says.

And a small but ugly part of the story of Order No. 11, which followed an even more hideous chapter, the massacre of nearly 200 men and boys in Lawrence on Aug. 21.

"Tit for tat," as Potter says.

Most of those living in the counties of Jackson,

**Five ancestors of Bob Potter of Independence were killed in a mass shooting at Lone Jack in September 1863.** | KEITH MYERS, THE KANSAS CITY STAR

Cass, Bates and Vernon were given 15 days to get out of the area. Thousands, disloyal to the Union or not, were forced from their homes with only what could be carried, leaving crops in the fields, animals in the pastures.

Federal troops and Missouri militias then ensured the area would be useless to guerrillas. In Cass County, population 10,000 in 1860, only 600 people remained, mostly in Harrisonville and Pleasant Hill.

But not everyone even got the chance to leave.

Troopers of the 9th Kansas Cavalry arrived from Pleasant Hill and began gathering up men, some who were in the act of loading wagons and finding the oxen to pull them.

Eight were taken to the Federals' camp on the Roupe farm. Two could produce oaths of Union loyalty. The other six were gunned down by orders of Capt. Charles Coleman.

The Kansas troopers may have been carrying a grudge. Three months earlier, two of their companies had been ambushed just south of Westport; 16 were killed. More likely, though, they saw it as just revenge for helping William Quantrill and his men on their way to Lawrence.

The guerrillas, the story goes, had been well provisioned from Ben Potter's smokehouse, with other food donated by his neighbors. The Potters' oats also went to feed the 300 bushwhackers' horses.

"They didn't know where Quantrill and his men were going or what they were going to do," Potter believes. "How could they?"

He says they "would have helped anybody who'd come through hungry and needing a place to stay."

The area was decidedly secessionist. The dead men had kin serving in the rebel army in Arkansas.

Slave owners, Potter says.

"They only would have had a few to help work the farms. This was hemp country. Hemp farming was hard work."

Potter, 82, a retired auctioneer, sits in a recliner in the living room of his Independence home across from his wife, Ruth. She prompts him on details he

A stone dove once graced the top of this monument in the Six-Man Cementery near Long Jack.

leaves out.

Graves were quickly dug. Would the Yankees return? No time to make caskets. The women, four of them freshly widowed, one seven months pregnant, wrapped the bodies in bed quilts.

They told the more than two dozen frightened children to climb into the wagons or walk away from the wheels. The oxen were whipped into slow motion and the refugees began wending their way east.

There's yet another refugee in Potter's family history — on his mother's side.

One morning, Potter told about 50 Civil War enthu-

siasts at the Midwest Genealogy Center in Independence: "When Order No. 11 was issued, Laura Harris Flannery Bridges — that was my great-grandmother — was forced to leave her home near what is now Hickman Mills."

"A tough lady," he says.

With her husband away in the rebel army, she put her son and some belongings in a wagon and, leading its team of oxen, walked to Sherman, Texas. She was in her mid-20s.

Soon widowed, she resettled and remarried in Jackson County after the war.

"She was courageous and had strong willpower," says Barbara Hughes, an Independence historian, who donned a 19th century dress and bonnet to play the role of Bridges at an event at the genealogy center.

"When she got to Lone Jack, Bridges, in an interview she gave in 1929 to the Independence Examiner, said she heard gunshots ring out," Hughes says.

Old stories like that keep the fizz and the flavor of the Civil War alive. Another is that the Federal lieutenant colonel could not bear to witness the executions and disappeared into the brush for a while. And that Martin Rice and his son, the two men released, were informers and had perhaps fingered the other captives. That's mostly discounted now.

And there's the one of how some of the Caves came home from the war and intended to do something about the little massacre. They located Coleman, supposedly, and were making plans for a bit more tit for tat when the unhappy news came.

The cold-blooded captain had died, so goes the old family telling, "before we got to kill him."

# Civil War at 150: The past in the present?

**W**hy can't we just get over the Civil War in America?

Why does it still have such a hold on our imagination, on our political habits and rhetoric, on the stories through which we define ourselves as a people and a nation?

Why is the Confederacy, a mere four-year experiment in revolution to preserve a slaveholding society, still so interesting to so many people?

Haven't we had at least two "Reconstructions" — the first of the 1860s and '70s, the second the civil rights movement a century later — to solve those issues at the war's roots?

As we commemorate this most pivotal and transforming event — at the same time the country descends into some of the worst political polarization in modern times — it is important to visit these ques-

**AUTHOR'S ESSAY**
David W. Blight teaches American history at Yale University and is the author of the just released "American Oracle: The Civil War in the Civil Rights Era," as well as the multiple-award-winning "Race and Reunion: The Civil War in American Memory."

tions. The stakes are very high.

And, ideologically, many of the issues of 2011 are much the same as in 1861.

Given the hold the tea party seems to have on the base of the Republican Party, we should take notice when some in the group invoke the Confederate constitution as a model for anti-tax, anti-centralization libertarianism.

First, it was modeled closely after the U.S. Constitution. Second, its advocates may need a reminder of just how desperately the Jefferson Davis administration struggled to forge a centralized government out of the chaos of war, jealous localism, states' rights and homegrown greed and individualism.

Indeed, yesterday's secessionists and today's nullifiers have much in common. Both are distinct minorities who have suddenly seized an inordinate degree of power.

One acted in revolution to save a slaveholders' republic; the other seems determined to render modern federal government all but obsolete for any purpose but national defense.

Both claim their mantle of righteousness in the name of "liberty," privatization and racial exclusion (one openly, the other using code that keeps it largely a white people's party). Both vehemently claim the authority of the "Founders."

Compromise? Both professed disinterest, indeed seemed to welcome rupture.

All this we might have thought all but buried in the mass slaughter of the Civil War. But, alas, history keeps happening.

Texas Gov. Rick Perry chose to announce his presidential candidacy in Charleston, S.C., where secession and the Civil War began.

Merely coincidental? This is the man who in 2009 suggested his state might consider "secession" as resistance to federal authority.

Perry crafted this line for his now larger national audience: "I'll work every day to try to make Washington, D.C., as inconsequential in your life as I can."

What would the United States be if Abraham Lincoln's administration and the federal government had decided to be "inconsequential" in 1861?

Texas secessionists would have realized their dream back then.

But how would have West Texas farmers in Depression-era Haskell County — where Perry grew up — have gotten electrification but from a consequential federal government?

Just how would racial segregation have been dismantled there or the rest of the country?

And would we prefer to have federal standards less consequential for food and drugs? Or how many national parks would there be if the feds had simply never bothered to be consequential in land use and natural resources. What kind of air might we be breathing if there were no Clean Air Act?

Interstate highways? Social Security? Workplace safety? College loans and the GI Bill, which helped forge an American middle class? An endless list.

We all make the past useful to our personal present, some more than others who might negate a social contract with their fellow humans in the service of private "freedom."

Is it possible that at the heart of this dispute is that the federal government — however cumbersome amid the arcs of history bending forward and backward — has actually been a vehicle for the increase of democracy and equality, and that some Americans resent this?

We live in a society in 2011 not only divided over race and the advent of a black president, over the rights of immigrants, over religious tolerance, over a seemingly permanent state of war, over who and what are legitimate Americans and whether they shall be accorded birthright citizenship.

And we have ceaseless debate about the proper relation of federal to state power.

That "Union" preserved by the Civil War generation, turning 150 years old, is not a healthy organism.

Yes, the Civil War is rooted in states' rights. But the significance of any exercise of states' rights, like any other constitutional doctrine, is always in the issue to which it is employed.

Today, states' rights claims are advanced by many governors and Republican-majority legislatures in the very language of "secession" and "nullification" made so infamous in antebellum America. They are aided and abetted by a conservative majority on the Supreme Court, although the justices have not justified "nullification" by name.

What indeed has brought those words back into our political parlance?

A short list of examples among many tells us just how alive some Civil War legacies are in our time.

Kentucky has a bill pending to make that state a "sanctuary" from the Environmental Protection Agency. Arizona Republicans want to exempt products made in their state from federal interstate commerce laws. Montana has one bill that would "nullify" the federal Endangered Species Act and another to require the FBI to get a local sheriff's permission to make any arrests.

Contexts change, of course, but we have a history with these ideas, and it had a terrible result in 1861.

Put most directly, either the United States reborn in slave emancipation is based on a social contract, forged and reforged by the new historical imperatives of industrialization and urbanization in the Progressive era and by a horrible economic Depression in the 1930s and a civil rights revolution of the 1960s, all of which for real reasons necessitated the increased exercise of federal power to protect human liberty, welfare and survival, or it is not.

The conservative movement in America, or at least its most radical wing, seems determined to repeal much of the 20th century and even its constitutional and social roots from the transformative 1860s.

The Civil War is not only not over, it can still be lost. As the sesquicentennial ensues in publishing and conferences and on television and countless websites, one can hope that we will pursue matters of legacy and memory with one eye on the past and the other acutely on the present.

The stakes are high.

# WHEN SLAVERY AND A FREE PRESS COLLIDED, VIOLENCE OFTEN ENSUED

By **DARRYL LEVINGS** ★ THE KANSAS CITY STAR

At one point, during the Civil War, The New York Times installed a Gatling gun on its roof to deal with the anti-draft riots.

Ah, those were the days.

Many of the smaller newspapers in our region probably wished they had been so equipped. Back then, it was de-rigueur for critical readers to dump the type and press, if not the editor, in the nearest river.

In much of America, newspapering was booming. Nearly 4,000 dailies or weeklies cranked off hand presses in small towns or off the steam-powered rotary machines in places like New York, home of the famous and powerful three, the Herald, Tribune and Times.

But where slavery rubbed up against a free press, violence was often sparked.

In 1855, a pro-slavery gang calling itself the Platte County Self-Defensive Association mob attacked the Parkville Industrial Luminary for its stance against the Border Ruffians — Missourians going into Kansas for intimidation or ballot stuffing. The paper was declared "a nuisance, which has been endured too long, and should now be abated."

The press and some of the type ended in the Missouri River, and a co-editor barely escaped tar and feathering. The other editor, George Park, for whom the town and college is named, was luckily out of town; the surviving type was smuggled into Kansas.

The next year, hundreds of Missourians rode into Lawrence to deal with, among other things, the "nuisances" of two abolitionist newspapers.

"The newspaper offices were the first objects of attack," Thomas H. Gladstone, a passing Englishman, wrote home. "First that of the Free State, then that of the Herald of Freedom, underwent a thorough demolition. The presses were in each case broken to pieces, and the offending type carried away to the river. The papers and books were treated in like manner, until the soldiers became weary of carrying them to the Kaw, when they thrust them in piles into the street, and burnt, tore, or otherwise destroyed them."

Years later, William Quantrill burned the next generation of Lawrence papers: the Journal, Tribune and Republican. It would be more than a month before the

Journal struggled back into business. In an earlier raid on Olathe, Quantrill's men also attacked the presses of the Herald and the Mirror.

The Southern sentiment in Kansas City in the war's early months drove most of its papers — the weekly Enquirer, a German weekly called the Missouri Post, and the Free State Republican — out of business or into Kansas.

Even the Journal of Western Commerce briefly ceased publication for lack of support.

Not surprisingly, most reporting in Missouri was strongly pro-Union, not surprisingly since all the towns were occupied by Federal troops. One exception was in Independence, at least until August 1862 when the 6th Kansas Cavalry rode in.

"My first act was to place under arrest McCarty, the editor of the Border Star, a secession paper ... and a lying, dirty sheet," reported Maj. Wyllis Ransom. "Having no means at hand of removing the material, I ordered the type of the office to be destroyed."

Another Democratic paper, the Leavenworth Inquirer, was wrecked by a mob incited by its "Cop-

**Leslie's Illustrated did a little self promoting, depicting in one of its engravings Federal soldiers perusing its editions for the latest war news back in camp.**

| FRANK LESLIES' ILLUSTRATED HISTORY OF THE CIVIL WAR, COURTESY OF THE MISSOURI VALLEY ROOM, KANSAS CITY LIBRARY

perhead" views.

But that left no shortage of stinging editorials in Leavenworth, where the Daily Times and the Daily Conservative daily tried to kick the other's teeth in. The Times, a moderate Republican paper, hated Sen. James Lane, who controlled the more radical Conservative. Lane hated back.

On Sept. 4, 1864, the Times reported that Lane tried to raise a mob to destroy its offices the night before: "Beautiful business for a United States Senator! We can inform Lane that destroying a loyal paper will prove a very different business from destroying a disloyal one. Let him and his minions make that issue before the people of this State if they choose."

The Conservative had been founded by Daniel Read Anthony, whose bravery was impugned by Robert Saterlee of the Herald. They met in the street with revolvers, and Leavenworth quickly was minus one editor.

Anthony, briefly a top officer with the 7th Kansas Cavalry, was an original jayhawker, a connoisseur of stolen Missouri horse flesh — and a man quick with a match.

Having practiced on Missouri towns, Anthony, once elected Leavenworth mayor, burned out homes of the town's Southern sympathizers. He also had a Times editor arrested for "disturbing the peace," that is, printing an article critical of Union Gen. Joseph Hooker.

Another journalistic jack-of-all-trades was down river in Kansas City. Robert Van Horn, an owner of the Journal of Western Commerce, got elected mayor in 1861 and then organized a battalion that he took to the Battle of Lexington. There he was wounded, paroled and went on to fight again at Shiloh.

In 1864, as Maj. Gen. Sterling Price's Confederates marched toward Kansas, the Leavenworth Times insisted Price had turned back south. This led many Kansas militiamen to turn mutinous, believing their call-out a political trick by Lane to keep them from ballot boxes in coming elections back home.

"Am of the opinion that the paper should be temporarily suspended, and editors and writers arrested as enemies to the public and cause," an alarmed Federal provost marshal telegraphed to a commander. "Please instruct. Course of paper is highly treasonous at this time."

Once Price was beaten below Westport, the Journal opined on the rebels they saw, dead or captured: "They seem to belong to a different race from ours, and most certainly to an inferior one. In truth, this war is one of intelligence, enlightened, and Christian civilization against barbarism."

The war over, some of those same rebels, Maj. John Edwards and Col. John Moore, tried to enlighten Kansas City readers with their own Kansas City Times. The two men, adjutants to rebel generals Jo Shelby and John Marmaduke, are remembered in part for their sympathy to the James brothers, former Missouri brush rebels turned to banditry.

Other papers defied Radical Republican rule. The masthead of The Unterrified Democrat of Linn, Mo., still survives; that of the Lexington Caucasian, fortunately, does not.

For editors, the post-war period seemed almost as dangerous as to bank tellers.

The hot-headed Anthony was horsewhipped by an angry mayor and nearly shot to death at the opera by another editor. His sister, Susan B., helped hold the bandage to his neck in the critical days.

But not all editor scrapes turned out so bloody.

Edwards left Kansas City for a time to become an editor of the St. Louis Times. There he challenged Emory Foster, editor of the St. Louis Journal, to a duel in 1875. The cause? Foster had called Edwards a liar for claiming Jefferson Davis was mistreated at an Illinois fair.

Foster, the Union commander badly wounded at the Lone Jack battle, traded first shots with Edwards, who himself had taken a slug in fighting at Cape Girardeau.

"A little high," Foster calmly noted of Edwards' first round.

"I will go on if it takes a thousand fires," Edwards declared, but his foe insisted that honor had been upheld.

So the wordsmiths shook hands and, with some bourbon — nearly as crucial as ink to an editor of the day — made an early-morning toast.

Old solders, in a fading group photograph, taken at Gettysburg in 1913. Confederate soldiers, survivors all. Among them, Thomas C. Holland, with a scar on his cheek and a story that his great-great-grandson, Kurt Holland, 50, of Missouri City, loves to tell. His ancestor, a lieutenant in the 28th Virginia Regiment, served in Pickett's division in the great battle, where he was wounded and captured. After the war, Holland settled in Kansas City, but traveled back to Gettysburg for the big 50-year reunion of old soldiers. Wandering to the spot he'd reached in the doomed charge against Cemetery Ridge, 50 years earlier, he found another old man there, a veteran of Cushing's Battery of Philadelphia, which had done its part in chewing up the Virginians. They Yankee was telling his wife of killing a rebel there, one he still felt bad about; the foe was plainly crazy, waving his hat and hollering, "Come on boys!" Holland pointed at his cheek, where the slug had slammed into his face, then the back of his head, where it exited. "I am the man you killed, but I am a pretty lively corpse." They shook hands, became friends and exchanged letters for years.

*"I am the man you killed, but I am a pretty live corpse."*

# CIVIL WAR 150 TRIVIA BATTLE

By DARRYL LEVINGS ★ THE KANSAS CITY STAR

## THE ANSWERS

**1** The fictional Rooster Cogburn of "True Grit" lost his eye in the fierce Battle of Lone Jack in southeast Jackson County.

**2** During a duel near Little Rock, Ark., Gen. John Sappington Marmaduke put a fatal revolver bullet into Gen. Lucius Walker's kidney. Marmaduke had asked to be assigned to a different commander, which was correctly interpreted by Walker as a reflection upon his courage. After hitting Walker with his second shot, Marmaduke, always the gentleman, did offer his ambulance.

**3** The stone in Woodlawn Cemetery in Independence says guerrilla chief George Todd died Oct. 23, 1864, the date of the Battle of Westport. Actually he was fatally shot in the neck after the Battle of the Little Blue on Oct. 21 and died that night or the next morning.

**4** The first area town to be linked by rails to the rest of the world was Weston in 1860, through the Platte Valley line, a spur down from the Hannibal & St. Joseph Railroad. A rail link between Wyandotte and Lawrence was operating by December 1864, but the "Iron Horse" did not reach Kansas City from St. Louis until September 1865.

**5** The Westport street named for a Civil War victim is Archibald Street, for Archibald Yoacham, killed at Wilson's Creek. He was the son of Daniel Yoacham, who operated the first tavern in the frontier hamlet in the 1820s.

**6** A long way from Missouri, Henry Hungerford Marmaduke commanded a gun crew on the CSS Virginia, also known as the Merrimack. He was wounded during the famous Hampton Roads battle with the USS Monitor. A younger brother of the general, the lieutenant attended the Naval Academy and is buried at Arlington Cemetery.

**7** James O'Neill, a part-time artist for Frank Leslie's Illustrated Newspaper, a New York-based publication, was killed at Baxter Springs, Kan. He was accompanying Maj. Gen. James Blunt south, riding in the wagon with the band, when their small Federal column was nearly wiped out by William Clarke Quantrill's guerrillas.

**FIRST BONUS:** Some might say the letters WPF on the Parrott gun in Loose Park denote it was made at the West Point Foundry. A good answer, but a Google answer and wrong. No letters are found on the tube of this gun, but you can tell the difference without them. Northern foundries left a sharp front edge on the band of reinforcing iron at the breech. For some reason, the Southern foundries beveled this edge.

**SECOND BONUS:** The Missourian to serve on both sides of the conflict was Maj. Manning Marius Kimmel, West Point class of 1857. After the battle of Bull Run, the Union officer got leave on the false story that his father was sick in Philadelphia, then went to Louisville, where he wrote his resignation from the U.S. Army. He became an ordnance officer in the Confederate army west of the Mississippi.